Scaling to Exit

Doubling the Valuation of Your Business

Michael A. Watkins, MBA/JD

Scaling to Exit

Michael Watkins
Cover design by Shane Gibbons:

Printed in the United States of America
ISBN-13: 978-1987566550
ISBN-10: 1987566556

While the author has made every effort to provide accurate Internet addresses at the time of publication, neither the publisher nor the author assumes any responsibility for errors or changes in third-party Internet addresses. Further, neither the publisher nor the author has any control over nor assumes any responsibility for third-party content.

Dedication

I have been incredibly blessed my entire life. I was born into a Christian home with absolutely amazing parents. My father, who is no longer with us, taught me many things, but what I value most is the way he modeled hard work and perseverance. My mother, who is a successful entrepreneur in Orlando, Florida, is the one who gave me a vision of who I could be.

I have been married for thirty-five years to the most amazing woman, and she is the mother of my two amazing and accomplished daughters. My father and these four women—my mother, my wife, and my two daughters—are the wind beneath me. I thank God for them.

Michael Watkins
Lafayette, Colorado

Contents

Foreword

Running your business with the end in mind is the new paradigm. Michael Watkins has given us a blueprint on how to do this. In *Scaling to Exit*, Michael provides an action plan that covers all of the essentials—those things that are often neglected by owners who are too busy running their business to work on their business. Whether you are preparing to sell your business in 3–5 years or just starting up, his framework is a valuable tool that will increase profits and the value of your business. Very few owners realize a "greater than imagined" return on their investment. *Scaling to Exit* provides owners with a plan that will help them watch others increase the bottom-line value of their dreams. This is a must-read for every business owner.

Mark Inboden
President/CEO
Utility Control & Equipment Corporation

Introduction

There is light at the end of the tunnel, but unfortunately it is the headlights of an oncoming train. And the train looks like this:

- There are approximately 4 million businesses with employees owned by Baby Boomers in the United States.

- For the greatest majority of these business owners, 80-90 percent of their retirement assets are in the form of the business itself.

- Statistically, fewer than 20 percent of these Boomers are going to successfully sell their business.

  These statistics are consistent with BizBuySell's (www.BizBuySell.com) most recent national report, which indicated that about one of every five listings (20 percent) on the online marketplace for small business sales and purchases had closed a sales transaction in 2016.

There is an inevitable train wreck on the 3–5-year horizon for an incredibly large segment of the US population, the impact of which will be felt for generations. The question becomes this: Are you going to be a statistic, or are you going to take the steps necessary to unlock the promise that your company holds for your posterity and financial future?

What Should Baby Boomer Business Owners Do to Avoid the Train Wreck?

This book will be strong medicine to many; however, to extend the metaphor, sometimes it takes strong medicine to make you well.

This book was written for the business owner who desires to successfully exit from their company in the next three to five years, and is seeking to increase the attractiveness of and at least double the valuation of their company in that time frame.

It is intended to be short enough for the reader to decide if they see themselves in the value proposition (i.e., increasing the attractiveness of and doubling the valuation of their company), but long enough to provide the reader with insight into the heavy lifting required to achieve their goals. It is also intended to be provocative enough to inspire Baby Boomer business owners to get serious about taking control of their posterity and their financial future.

In the words of Hillel the Elder, a first-century Jewish scholar, "If I am not for myself, who will be for me? . . . If not now, when?"

The pertinent facts:

- It will likely take 2–3 years to make your business attractive for sale

- If you wait a couple of years to begin, it will still take 2–3 years to make your business attractive for sale

- If you have to *sell* your business, statistically you have less than a 20 percent chance of succeeding. To increase your chances of success, you want private equity or a strategic investor to *buy* your business. So let's make it happen!

The Exit Planning Institute (EPI) reports that it has been a seller's market for businesses since 2015, but that trend is attributed to unattractive supply rather than to strong demand. Multiples are historically high, but it is because private equity companies and strategic buyers don't have a lot of attractive businesses to pick from. There are simply not enough high-quality businesses for sale for smart money to buy, which clearly defines your opportunity!

So how does one make one's business such that private equity and/or a strategic investor will want to buy it? There is no silver-bullet solution. It requires an investment in the development and execution of an exit plan that ensures that future buyers will view your business as distinctive and valuable.

The Scaling to Exit Program

The *Scaling to Exit* Program is just such an exit plan.

The program features an online assessment that allows you, the business owner, to accurately gauge the strength of your company in five critical areas:

1. Marketing
2. Sales
3. Operations
4. Finance
5. Management

Based on the assessment results, a custom strategy for "scaling" your business is developed.

The primary differentiator of the *Scaling to Exit* program compared to others is assistance in the execution of the strategy. We don't just tell you what you should do and wish you the best of luck. We commit a corporate development resource to your strategy execution who becomes an extension of your executive management team. The corporate development resource is defined in more detail in the appendix, but the role coordinates his/her efforts with those of the *Scaling to Exit* program support team to project manage the movement of your company towards your exit goals.

Core Team	Fractional C-suite
• Corporate Development Resource • Business Attorney • CPA/ Valuation Expert • Business Broker	• Chief Marketing Officer (CMO) • Vice President Sales • Chief Financial Officer (CFO) • Chief Operations Officer (COO) • Learning & Development

Scaling to Exit Program support team

Note that the *Scaling to Exit* program fractional C-suite resources are professionals who offer their advice and skills to organizations on a for-hire basis. These executives have served in business for many years in roles such as chairman, owner, director, CxO, SVP, and VP. Some have skills focused in one discipline, while others have a broad base of knowledge and experience. *Scaling to Exit* program fractional resources are not employees; they offer their services to many companies simultaneously. Because they serve many clients in multiple industries, they provide diverse perspectives that have an immediate impact on client companies.

Size Makes a Difference

Size makes a difference, so scalability is at the core of the *Scaling to Exit* program.

The International Business Broker Association (IBBA) and M&A Source, in partnership with the Pepperdine University, recently summed up survey results from 250 respondents about businesses being marketed and sold in the United States. The data was drawn from businesses listed for sale and/or sold during the second quarter of 2014, from "Main Street" (defined as those companies with a value up to $2 million), as well as from the "Lower Middle Market" (defined as those with a value between $2 million and $50 million). The graphic on the next page summarizes their findings.

Quarter 2, 2014
Data: IBBA | M&A Source | Pepperdine University

EBITDA Multiples Increase with Size

The chart exhibits the fact that the underlying median EBITDA (Earnings Before Interest, Taxes, Depreciation, and Amortization, or, "Operating Profits") multiple used to calculate the value and purchase price of a business on Main Street and in the Lower Middle Market increases with size.

Relatively speaking, if a business is on the upper end of the Main Street sector or in the Lower Middle Market sector, buyers considering the acquisition of the business will be more willing to increase the EBITDA multiple they use to assess its value. Simply stated, grow the size of your business and its value will increase in the eyes of a buyer.

Deal Terms Needed to Close the Sale

If you want to avoid having a buyer ask for seller financing, growing your business to a $5 million valuation will go a long way towards making that happen. In the IBBA/M&A Source survey, not one buyer sought seller financing when the business purchase price exceeded $5 million. On the other hand, for those businesses with purchase prices in the

$500,000 to $1 million range, nearly one out of every five buyers required the business seller to accept some portion of their payment in the form of a seller's note receivable.

It should also be noted that one half of all businesses with valuations between $5 million and $50 million were acquired by private equity firms, with the other half split between strategic buyers and existing business owners seeking new business opportunities.

The conclusion—grow ("scale") your enterprise! If at all possible, scale your business to a minimum valuation of $5 million. That is the objective of the *Scaling to Exit* program.

Shall We Get Started?

This is the question I ask business owners after we have presented the value proposition and walked through the *Scaling to Exit* program. It is important to understand that, conservatively, there will be 4 million Baby Boomers seeking to exit their companies in the next 3–5 years. Realistically, our firm will only be able to support 40–50 of those companies. The clock is ticking! There are so many companies and so little time.

I remember six or seven years ago meeting with the owners of one of the larger sign companies on the front range of Colorado. They wanted to sell the business and retire on the proceeds. Over the course of several meetings, I developed a high-level understanding of the business and the challenges it faced. It was a typical scenario: the husband and wife owned and managed every aspect of the business. They never took a vacation because they couldn't leave the business in the hands of their employees. They had little documentation and no succession plan for staffing their replacements. I had to break the news to them that the business held very little value for a potential buyer.

When owner(s) are integral to the business's value proposition, they are typically not surprised to hear that their company holds very little value for a potential buyer unless their retention is a component of the sale. What does surprise most owners is how comprehensive the required change is to get their company on the right track. The sign company owners, for example, were overwhelmed by our prescription. They were simply unwilling to make the investment of time and resources necessary to turn their company into an attractive acquisition target. I subsequently learned from a local workman's compensation broker that the husband unfortunately ended up with a terminal illness and the wife was forced to shut down the business and sell the inventory and equipment to a competing sign company at fire-sale prices.

It didn't have to end that way for the sign company. If they had begun executing the *Scaling to Exit* program six or seven years ago, they may have had an opportunity for a healthy exit. They may have netted enough from the sale of the company to comfortably provide for the wife in her retirement. These folks are only two people in a long line of business owners who don't appreciate the fact that doing nothing is actually riskier than making the investment to do something.

It is often said that most people are capable of dealing with adversity, but few can cope effectively with success. The psychology behind this fact is beyond the scope of this book, but the truthfulness of the statement deserves attention. The underlying fact is this: You can buy almost everything today. You can buy ideas, knowledge, materials, and resources. You can even buy (the use of) money. The only thing you cannot buy is the courage, commitment, and persistence required to pursue a vision of maximizing the valuation of your company.

Maybe this inability to cope effectively with success is the explanation behind the fact that "the seller had a change of heart…" is far and away the number one reason that business sell transactions "go south". A change of heart that can be traced back to the owner's emotional attachment to their business. This would suggest that the most important exit plan is the plan for what you are going to be after you exit!

Many intermediaries will refuse to take a listing from sellers who have no clear idea of what they will be doing after the sale. Such sellers are much more likely to find excuses to delay a sale, make unreasonable demands, or simply grenade the deal as the closing date approaches.

The balance of this book is going to be about the transactional activities associated with making a business attractive to a potential buyer and doubling its valuation in three to five years. All of these activities belong in the cognitive domain – the "knowing" domain. You can "know" what it is that needs to be done in order to execute on the transactional activities, and you can "buy" the talent that you will need to augment your existing staff in that pursuit. In this way, the transactional activities really represent the relatively "easy stuff".

The heavy lifting occurs when you are forced into the affective domain – the "emotional" domain. The place that you will have to be when you contemplate the answer to the question "what's next after the sale of your company?" To contemplate the answer to the question, not in terms of what you will <u>do</u>, but rather in terms of what you will <u>be</u>. It will be amazingly gratifying to develop and execute a plan around the answer to that question.

Its not about contentment

One thing is for certain; what you will be should not be about contentment. Many business owners are under the impression that the sale of their business is going to generate enough cash for them to be content. That once they are no longer under the weight and pressure of running a company on a day-to-day basis, that they will be content. Well... it almost never ends up that way. Contentment isn't all that it is made out to be.

I remember maybe ten years ago, being on a consulting engagement in Philadelphia at the facilities of a Fortune 50 client. I was assisting this corporation, which was comprised of more than 140 individual companies, consolidate seven of their companies into one larger company. All seven of these companies had a common federal client, so it made really good economic sense to combine them. Unfortunately, it also meant that six executives were being compelled to surrender their President titles. I was there to help these executives with that transition (affective domain stuff). I had the participants off in an exercise when the vice president of human resources made the observation that all of the gentlemen in the group were going to retire in the next 5 years. Then she asked me a really interesting question. She asked me how many [monthly] checks on average will the corporation have to write to each one of them in their retirement.

I thought about the question for a moment and hazarded a guess that they would probably receive checks for 15 years on average. So I responded with approximately 180 checks. To my surprise, she said that they would write 37 checks on average...37 checks! I decided right then that I would never retire and seek contentment. It appears that very little good comes out of being retired and content.

The pursuit of your passion

I am proposing an alternative to contentment. I am proposing the pursuit of your passion. If we can identify your passion, then we can identify the source of courage that will enable you to become all that you have yet to become. This is one of the things that makes the *Scaling to Exit* program so complete. The first step that we take is to help you to explore the question of what will you be after the sale of your business.

Jerry Garcia, lead guitarist and vocalist with the band the Grateful Dead, said, "Our audience is like people who like licorice. Not everybody likes licorice, but the people who like licorice really like licorice." It has been our experience that a similar thing holds true for business owners. Not every business owner has the courage to intentionally create a successful exit plan, but the business owners who do have that courage, have a ton of it. For business owners who have little or no exit planning in place, courage will need to become an acquired taste (especially if 80–90 percent of their financial assets are tied up in the business).

A Vision for How It Could Be

I have a good friend and client with whom I began working in 2001. This gentleman, who we will refer to as Bill, had a 20-person CNC manufacturing business when I first met him. Back then, he did virtually everything—he was the salesperson, he oversaw the manufacturing operations, and he handled all client and personnel issues. He was the prototypical business stakeholder/ owner/ founder/ inventor that we reference throughout this book as "business owner."

Even though he was relatively young, I asked Bill for a description of his exit plan. I explained that an exit plan that included selling the business to a non-strategic buyer was already in jeopardy because he represented the greatest asset in the business. In other words, without him, the business was worth little more than the salvage value of the equipment. So we began, way back then, to design and execute a strategy for making the business autonomous. We staffed it with human resources, and then coached and mentored them to the point that they were capable of operating the business on a daily basis.

Today, Bill's business is a highly profitable 68-person enterprise, and it continues to grow at an impressive clip. Bill spends 3–4 months per year at his second home in Florida and enjoys a new role as an executive in an industry organization that he has belonged to for 30 years. The business is so strong and profitable that he receives generous offers to purchase it on a monthly basis. Bill had a vision, but more importantly, he had the courage to execute a plan for achieving that vision. Interestingly, because the business is autonomous and generates healthy cash flow, Bill sees no reason to exit from it anytime soon.

One

The Scaling to Exit Program

The lion's share of the 4 million Baby Boomer business owners will retire in the next five to seven years. The vast majority of them have 80–90 percent of their financial assets tied to the business they hope to sell. In reality, fewer than 20 percent of these business owners will succeed in selling their business for a price that will fund their retirement.

The numbers are staggering. If we assume that, starting today, these 4 million companies went up for sale in an orderly, linear fashion, it would mean that companies would hit the market at a torrential rate of 48,000–67,000 per month!

Obviously 4 million companies will not go up for sale in an orderly, linear fashion. It is impossible to accurately predict what the actual trend will be, but it is interesting to speculate about three conceivable scenarios.

Scenario #1

20 percent of Baby Boomer-owned companies go on the market in the next three years (20/80 ratio—where 20 percent of the 4 million companies go for sale in the next three years and 80 percent after three years).

Scenario #2

30 percent of Baby Boomer-owned companies go on the market in the next three years (30/70 ratio).

Scenario #3

40 percent of Baby Boomer-owned companies go on the market in the next three years (40/60 ratio).

Based on the ratios above, the numbers would look something like this:

	# of COs for sale	
Ratio	≤ 3 yrs	> 3yrs
20/80	800,000	3,200,000
30/70	1,200,000	2,800,000
40/60	1,600,000	2,400,000

The best-case scenario is that "only" 20 percent of Baby Boomer-owned companies go on the market in the next three years **and** you are able to **make** your company an attractive target to potential buyers within that timeframe. This scenario offers the least amount of competition, but even this best-case scenario contemplates some 22,000 companies hitting the market every month.

The worst-case scenario is that "only" 20 percent of Baby Boomer-owned companies go on the market in the next 3 years **and** you **miss** that window because you were unable to make your company an attractive target to potential buyers in that timeframe.

Truthfully, none of the scenarios beyond three years look very good.

The *Scaling to Exit* program was developed to partner with a select number of companies in their efforts to double their valuation and dramatically increase their attractiveness to buyers. The *Scaling to Exit* approach and methodology has to be radical and groundbreaking because these are radical and groundbreaking times. Millions of Baby Boomer business owners are on a path that will leave them with an insufficient nest egg for their retirement. The *Scaling to Exit* program seeks to rescue as many owners as possible from such a fate.

The Team

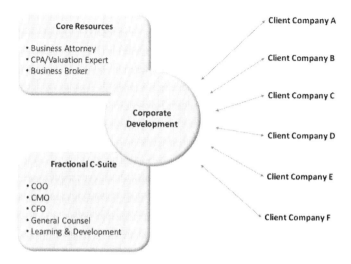

The Scaling to Exit support team includes core resources who are the usual participants in any business transaction:

- Business Attorney
- CPA/ Valuation Expert
- Business Broker

The difference between our approach and the approach of others is that our core team will be in place at client companies for up to three years before the actual sell transaction. This enables us to provide advice and counsel on how to best prepare the company for sale. In other words, the *Scaling to Exit* support team is not just a referral network. It is a talented and experienced group of professionals who the client company has engaged in order to generate economies of scale.

The organization chart below provides a general list of C-level roles. Not every company has a need for every C-level role, but ignorance is *not* bliss if your company does have a need for a particular C-level role and it is overlooked.

A company that is seeking to double its valuation absolutely has a need for a majority of the C-suite disciplines. The problem is they don't have a need for them on a full-time basis. A fractional C-suite is an effective alternative to incurring something on the order of $125K+ of monthly expense to hire a full-time C-suite. Instead of paying for a full-time C-suite, a company can pay for a fraction of a C-suite—a fraction that can be as low as 10 percent. This is a manageable investment that allows a company to gain access to the talent that will be required to turbo-charge growth, attractiveness, and valuation.

Vibrant and growing companies share some commonalities, and among the most important of those is having access to senior-level marketing and sales resources, an experienced corporate attorney, and a senior-level information systems professional. In other words, the C-suite disciplines are critical for sustained growth and success.

Before the advent of the fractional C-suite concept, a company that couldn't afford full-time C-suite professionals would have to engage these resources on an as-needed, ad-hoc basis. As issues arose, the flaws in this approach became evident. Consider the following:

1. A critical issue arises, and the business owner assumes that he/she knows enough to make an informed decision. Of course, no one is expert in every discipline, and every business owner has blind spots. In time, these blind spots can lead to poor and costly decision-making. But without C-suite help, who else is there to make a better decision? No one. Being a business owner is extremely lonely.

2. A critical issue arises, and the business owner contracts the help of a C-suite. Not only will this be expensive, it will be time consuming. C-suite professionals will spend (and bill for) valuable time orienting themselves with the business and the specific issue before commencing any problem solving. Should time be of the essence, the business owner may find himself hard pressed to make a strong decision, even with the assistance of a C-suite.

The business owner that is under way with the *Scaling to Exit* program has a fractional C-suite. They are no longer going it alone. Their fractional C-suite is engaged with the business on a regular basis. No money will be spent bringing these professionals up to speed, because they are already familiar with the ins and outs of your company. As a result, there is a high likelihood that the combined leadership team has enough knowledge to quickly and effectively make an informed decision about any issue the company may encounter.

I often encourage clients to read the book *Millionaire Next Door*, a nationwide best-seller by Thomas Stanley and William Danko. In the book, the authors debunk the myths surrounding millionaires and provide readers with a fascinating examination of the common characteristics of "everyday" millionaires. What they found, amongst other things, was that many people who live in upscale neighborhoods and drive luxurious cars do not have extreme wealth. Conversely, many people who have great wealth do not live in upscale neighborhoods. The book is a must-read because it provides practical insights into what the average person can do to become wealthy.

The sequel to the *Millionaire Next Door* is a book entitled *The Millionaire Mind*. This book examines a population of millionaires who have accumulated substantial wealth (deca-millionaires, or people worth $10 million or more). In exploring the ideas, beliefs, and behaviors that enabled these millionaires to build and maintain their fortunes, Dr. Stanley uncovered the concept of a "personal board of directors." He describes a personal board of directors as a small group of people who the financial elite leverage for their decision-making. Here is the premise:

- In an area in which I have little knowledge and/or expertise, if left to my own devices, I have considerably less than a 50 percent chance of making a good decision.

- If I run my idea/decision by one other [smart] person, we may get my chances of success to 50 percent, but not much more.

- If I run my idea/decision by 4–5 other [smart] people, my chances of making a good decision climb so astronomically that it would be difficult for me to make a bad decision.

Substitute deca-millionaire for business owner, and you begin to see the value of the fractional C-suite. Go it alone, and the average [smart] owner has a less than 50 percent chance of increasing the attractiveness and doubling the valuation of his/her company. Gather a C-suite of smart people, and you almost cannot fail.

When a bona-fide issue is identified by the combined team, then there is a high likelihood that one or more of the C-level resources will have the knowledge and expertise to address the issue. No additional time, energy, and expense is needed to craft a resolution. In the unlikely event that the knowledge and expertise is not present on the team, one or more of the C-level resources will certainly know where to source it. The fractional C-suite can leverage an extensive professional network to source the expertise at a reasonable rate.

Corporate Development Role

The corporate development resource is one of the game changers that makes the *Scaling to Exit* approach so radical. This retained resource becomes a member of the client company's leadership team. The owners of mid-tier companies are already running at full throttle. They do not have the margin to manage a fractional C-suite or execute on an EBITDA scaling strategy. The corporate development resource performs this role through twelve "sprints" per year with each client company.

The corporate development resource operates much like the CPU (central processing unit) of a computer. The CPU of a computer is efficient at swapping in and activating, and/or swapping out and deactivating, the resources that it requires to complete a task. In the same way, the corporate development resource is efficient at swapping in and activating, and/or swapping out and deactivating, the fractional C-suite resources that are required to make the *Scaling to Exit* program work at a client company.

How Does the Scaling to Exit Program Work?

Assessment	Strategy	Execution
• Sales & Marketing • Management • Business Model • Operations • Finance	• Scaling Approach • Goals/Objectives • Action Plan	• Implement the Program • 52 "Sprints" • Training & Development

The *Scaling to Exit* program is not intended to be a high-volume, low-touch proposition. It is intended to be just the opposite—an extremely high-touch experience for a select few client companies. The corporate development resource makes the high-touch experience a feasible approach for the entire team.

1. Assessment

The entire engagement begins with a formal assessment. It may be performed online, or the corporate development resource may interview the business owner (and his/her leadership team, if appropriate) in person. The interviews, and the ensuing discussions, focus on the Scaling to Exit functions that will produce the desired outcomes:

- Marketing
- Sales
- Operations
- Finance
- Management

The formal assessment also provides both parties with an opportunity to become familiar with one another. It is important to determine if there is enough compatibility for the parties to work together for 2–3 years. The product of the formal assessment is a detailed report that itemizes the findings of the corporate development resource and also lists the assumptions that will go into the preliminary valuation of the company.

2. Develop a Strategy for "Scaling" the Business

Assuming that there is compatibility between the parties, and that the business owner is serious about preparing the enterprise for an exit, the client company would register for the Scaling to Exit program.

The leadership team, led by the corporate development resource, will develop an EBITDA scaling strategy based on the findings in the assessment. The following scenarios represent the three pure strategies: (1) scaling EBITDA through revenue growth; (2) scaling EBITDA through gross profit growth (reduction in cost of goods sold), and (3) scaling EBITDA through operating expense reduction:

Scenario A	
Revenue Growth	100%
Gross Profit Growth	
Operating Expense Reduction	

Scenario B	
Revenue Growth	
Gross Profit Growth	100%
Operating Expense Reduction	

Scenario C	
Revenue Growth	
Gross Profit Growth	
Operating Expense Reduction	100%

In practice, the most executable EBITDA scaling strategies includes a combination of the three. These strategies incorporate a provision for modest but achievable revenue growth, a reduction in cost of goods sold, and a reduction in operating expense. The following graphic exhibits a typical scaling strategy:

Combination	
Revenue Growth	35%
Gross Profit Growth	40%
Operating Expense Reduction	25%

The leadership team will also devise a strategy for developing the management team and the finance/accounting function. While EBITDA growth is important to an increased valuation, the capability of the management team and the condition of the financials contribute mightily to the attractiveness of the company. This is so important that it is worth repeating: While EBITDA growth is important to an increased valuation, the capability of the management team and the condition of the financials contribute mightily to the attractiveness of the company.

3. Execute the Strategy

Project-Management Methodology

Studies have found that companies that use a standard project-management methodology have had fewer than half as many project failures as those that did not have one. This is why the *Scaling to Exit* team employs a version of Agile project management that is based on an incremental, iterative approach.

At the center of our project management approach is a scrum. A scrum is designed for teams of 3–9 resources who break their work into actions that can be completed within time-boxed iterations called sprints. In a sprint, a complete, useable, and potentially releasable work-product is created. Sprints have consistent durations throughout the *Scaling to Exit* program, and a new sprint starts immediately upon the conclusion of the previous sprint.

The corporate development resource keeps watch over the execution of the sprints. He/she limits sprints to one calendar month because when a sprint's horizon is too long, the definition of what is being implemented may change, complexity may rise, and risk may increase. Sprints provide the corporate development resource with predictability by ensuring inspection and adaptation, and they limit risk to one calendar month of cost.

Monitoring Execution

During the three-year engagement, the corporate development resource will bring a discipline of execution. We observe a cadence of weekly scrum meetings that relentlessly monitor the goals associated with the critical success factors that were identified in the *Scaling to Exit* strategy. The majority of weekly corporate-development-resource hours are dedicated to this pursuit.

How Much Does the Program Cost?

In an effort to acknowledge the challenges ahead, it is important to be as transparent as possible about how much it may cost to execute a *Scaling to Exit* program in your business.

Consider a fictitious $15 million manufacturer that we will call Mile-High Manufacturing (MHM). The financial data on the left describes MHM at the start of the *Scaling to Exit* program and the data on the right describes the business at exit.

At engagement		At Exit	
	Initial		Exit
Revenue	$ 15,000,000	Revenue	$20,101,435
EBITDA @ 10%	$ 1,500,000	EBITDA @ 15%	$ 3,015,215
Valuation @ 4.5 X EBITDA	$ 6,750,000	Valuation @ 4.5 X EBITDA	$ 13,568,468
Broker Fees @ 10%	$ 675,000	Broker Fees @ 5%	$ 678,423

- MHM was experiencing EBITDA of $1.5M or 10 percent of revenues

- MHM received a preliminary valuation of $6.75M ($1.5M x 4.5 = $6.75M)

  - The prevailing fees from brokering a business is 8–10 percent ($6.75M x .10 = $675,000)

The *Scaling to Exit* program would require an investment of approximately $300,000 over a three-year period for this $15 million business. The annual $100,000 is about 30 percent less than the cost of one senior executive, and instead of getting one executive, the client company gets the knowledge, skills, and abilities of an entire team of executives. In the referenced example, the *Scaling to Exit* program doubled the valuation of MHM through a combination of 10.25 percent year-over-year revenue growth and a 5 percent increase in gross profit. The result:

- MHM doubled its EBITDA from $1.5M to $3M

- MHM doubled its valuation from $6.75M to $13.5M

The net valuation gain of approximately $6.75 million represents a 22.5-times return on the $300,000 invested in the program.

Companies that register for the *Scaling to Exit* program typically agree to have our team broker the sale of their company. In return, we only charge a 5 percent fee for brokering the transaction. In the MHM example, the 5 percent broker fee of $678,423 would be one half of the $1,356,846 prevailing market rate of 10 percent. The savings to the business owner on broker fees at exit would be $678,423, which covers the cost of the *Scaling to Exit* program another 2.26 times.

Finally, the observant reader will also notice the $1.5M increase in EBITDA over that three-year period, which represents an additional 5.0-times return on the $300,000 invested.

Each engagement is different, but the following chart details how the approximately $300,000 required to execute the program is typically spent:

	Year 1	Year 2	Year 3
Corp Dev			
Retainer	$36,000	$36,000	$36,000
Training and Dev.	$10,000	$10,000	$10,000
CPA			
Audit	$3,000	$3,000	$3,000
Valuation	$2,000		
CMO			
Plan	$8,000		
3rd Party Labor	$30,000	$30,000	$30,000
CFO			
Plan	$2,000		
3rd Party Labor	$6,000	$6,000	$6,000
VP Sales			
Plan	$3,000		
3rd Party Labor	$10,000	$10,000	$10,000
Total	**$110,000**	**$95,000**	**$95,000**

Note that activities associated with executing actions for the various functions (i.e., sales, marketing, finance, and operations) may be self-performed by client company resources, if there is sufficient bandwidth and expertise within the organization to do so. If not, third-party resources would perform these functions for a fee.

Conclusion

Ernest Hemingway is one of my favorite authors. A quote that is widely attributed to him says, "There are only three sports: bullfighting, motor racing, and mountaineering; all the rest are merely games." Well, in the great game of business, the object is to generate as much profit as possible, while doing no harm.

A wonderful by-product of the *Scaling to Exit* program is winning the great game of business by accelerating organic growth to generate capital and increase valuations. Business owners win when they bring into being exit strategies that are so effective they accomplish the financial goal well before the three-year program runs its full course and become even more profitable after the three-year time frame.

Two

Scaling the Business Model

All things being equal, the most effective lever for dramatically increasing the valuation of a company is to scale it. The term "scaling" is used frequently in business, but it can have different meanings depending on the context in which it is used. For the purposes of this book, scaling may be defined as increasing revenue without experiencing a direct or one-to-one increase in operating costs.

Growing Versus Scaling

Generally, growing a business presumes that costs increase at a rate commensurate with the rate of revenue growth. The professional-services business model is the purest form of this kind of organizational growth. When this type of business gains a client, they hire more people to service the client, thus adding cost at the same rate in which they add revenue.

Scaling, on the other hand, is about adding revenue at a positive rate compared to added costs. Google is one example of a business that effectively scales. It adds customers at rate that outpaces the cost of the additional resources required to service those customers. This successful scaling is why they have been able to increase their margins at such a rapid rate in just a few short years.

Why is scaling so important? It provides the most leverage in the effort to at least double the valuation of client companies in three years.

Here is an example. Using the IBBA/M&A Source Association EBITDA multiples approach to valuation, let's take MHM, our fictitious $15 million manufacturer that has historically experienced an EBITDA of around 10 percent. MHM has received a preliminary valuation of 4.5 times EBITDA, or $6.75 million. MHM employed the Scaling to Exit program to double the preliminary valuation and achieve an exit valuation of $13.5 million. The team could accomplish this by "growing" the company or by "scaling" the company.

Grow		
	Preliminary	Exit
Revenue	$15,000,000	$30,000,000
EBITDA @10%	$1,500,000	$3,000,000
4.5 multiple	$6,750,000	$13,500,000

Scale		
	Preliminary	Exit
Revenue	$15,000,000	$20,101,435
EBITDA @15%	$1,500,000	$3,012,215
4.5 multiple	$6,750,000	$13,554,968

In the "grow" scenario, assuming a constant EBITDA of 10 percent, we would have to double the revenue (100 percent increase) in order to double the valuation of the company. In the "scale" scenario, we could double the value of the company with a much more modest 34 percent increase in revenue, when it is combined with an achievable 5 percent increase in EBITDA. Note that a 34 percent increase in revenue can be accomplished through a 10.25 percent year-over-year rate-of-revenue growth.

Scalability Is What Buyers Want

The goal of the Scaling to Exit program is to help you avoid the long odds associated with trying to sell your company. We do this by making it an attractive acquisition target for a strategic buyer or private equity group. So what do these types of buyers want in a company? There are three common responses to this question:

1. Scalability of the business model (operations)
2. Scalability of the management team
3. Scalability of marketing and sales

Scalability of the Business Model

For the purposes of this book, a business model will be defined as a company's plan for how it will generate revenue and make a profit from operations. The business model explains what products or services the business plans to manufacture and market, and how it plans to do so, including the expenses it will incur.

When analyst-types ask, "What's your business model?" they really want an answer to a much more basic and direct question: "How do you make money?"

A satisfactory answer to that question yields a long list of additional questions:

- Who's your target customer?

- What customer problem or challenge do you solve?

- What value do you deliver?

- How do you reach, acquire, and keep customers?

- How do you define and differentiate your offering?

- How do you generate revenue?

- What's your cost structure?

    - What are your working capital requirements?

    - What's your profit margin?

Good answers to these questions are critical to the scalability of a company's business model.

Gross Profit

Successful businesses have developed business models that enable them to fulfill client needs at a competitive price with sustainable costs. Over time, circumstances change, and businesses must revise their business models to reflect the changing environment and market demands, which may have limited the scalability of the former model. Many analysts use the gross profit metric as a way to compare the efficiency and effectiveness of competing business models. Gross profit is a company's total revenue minus the cost of goods sold (COGS).

For the business owner, the two primary levers of a company's business model are *pricing* and *cost*. To increase gross profit a company can 1) raise prices, 2) find direct materials, labor, and factory overhead at reduced costs, or 3) do a bit of each. Highly scalable businesses have high gross profit margins (over 50 percent), low support requirements, and minimal staffing.

Gross profit is often considered the first line of profitability because it only considers the cost of goods sold, not fixed operating expenses (i.e., general, administrative, and overhead). It focuses strictly on the way in which a company does business, not the efficiency of management (which we will discuss later). Investors who focus on business models leave room for an ineffective management team, because they believe that the best business models can scale and run themselves.

For example, consider two fictitious companies that rent and sell movies. Prior to the birth of the Internet, both companies made $5 million in revenue and the total cost of inventory sold was $4 million.

- Gross profit is calculated as $5 million - $4 million = $1 million.

- Gross profit margin is calculated as gross profit divided by revenue ($1 million ÷ $5 million = 0.20, or 20 percent).

After the advent of the Internet, one of the companies (Company B) decides to offer movies online instead of renting or selling physical copies. This change disrupts the business model in a positive way. The licensing fees do not change, but the cost of movie inventory is reduced considerably. In fact, the change reduces storage and distribution costs by $2 million.

- The new gross profit for Company B is $5 million - $2 million = $3 million.

- The new gross profit margin is 60 percent ($3 million ÷ $5 million = 0.60, or 60 percent).

Company B isn't generating more in sales, but it figured out a way to scale its business model in the changing environment, thus greatly reducing costs. Managers at company B enjoy an additional 40 percent in gross margin, while managers at company A have little room for error.

This example highlights a very important point. Even when companies are in the same or similar industries, there is something that allows one company to succeed over another. The secret begins and ends with how imaginatively each company approaches the first line of profitability—gross margin.

Is Your Business Service or Product Oriented?

When we collaborate with clients on developing a scaling strategy, the approach is based on one rudimentary distinction: is the client business service-oriented or product-oriented? One thing all good product-oriented businesses have in common is that they are inherently more scalable than even the best service-oriented companies. From a standpoint of scalability, clients who run service companies have already put themselves at a huge disadvantage. Service businesses are people oriented, making it harder to eliminate redundancies and increase automation. There are certainly steps service businesses can take to maximize efficiency, but in comparison to the scalability of a product business, service companies start off at a disadvantage.

Key Areas to Focus on in the Pursuit of a Scalable Business Model

Every business model is unique, and thus scalability is not a "one-size-fits-all" business strategy. Different industries require different approaches in order to reach more customers while controlling costs. That having been said, the Pareto Principle, also known as the 80/20 Rule, applies for every company, in every industry. The Pareto Principle states that 20 percent of your activities should account for 80 percent of your results. So, if there are ten items on your "To Do" list, two of those items should be worth five or ten times more than the other eight items put together.

The following activities represent the 20 percent that will account for 80 percent of your business model's scalability.

Establish Standardized and Repeatable Processes

When a company has three engineers, two founders, and a salesperson, it doesn't need a great deal of processes. When the team becomes 20 or 40 engineers, a group of product managers, and a formal senior management team, it is absolutely critical to have processes that standardize workflow, communication, and responsibilities, because flexibility can be the enemy of scalability and growth. If a company is going to scale, managers need to implement standardized and repeatable processes.

When a buyer seeks to purchase a business, they want to buy a system for making money that has a high likelihood of making more money under their ownership. This is particularly true for the private equity buyer. The buyer's perception of risk, and therefore their confidence in the likelihood of the business making money under their ownership, is affected by the existence of repeatable processes across every aspect of the business.

The graphic below presents an organizational alignment model that provides a construct for describing the importance of repeatable processes.

The "True North" of the model is the *Vision/Strategy*.

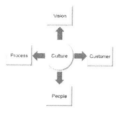

The model's Southern pole is *People*. It is people (employees) who execute the strategy that has been developed by the executive team. In his best-selling book

Good to Great, Jim Collins talks about getting the right people on the bus and into the right seats, and getting the wrong people off the bus. The *People* pole is all about getting the right people on the bus and into the right seats.

The Eastern pole is the *Customer.* Without delighted customers, a company will not survive. In order to grow, a founder must identify a value proposition that can be institutionalized within the business.

The Western pole—*Process*—is located opposite the *Customer* pole because an institutionalized value proposition, replete with well-developed and effective processes, increases the likelihood of achieving a delighted customer constituency. Without repeatable processes, a company relies upon "heroes"—typically the founder and 2–3 long-term employees—to produce delighted customers. This may be sufficient for a company with fewer than twenty employees and five clients, but it is not sustainable for a company with 50–60 people and twenty clients.

A process is a group of interrelated tasks that happen as a result of an event. These tasks produce a desired result for the customer, as an alternative to having the organization rely upon "heroes." Every business that is seeking efficiencies in order to facilitate profitable growth should develop a competency of mapping its core processes. Process mapping is an effective method for establishing repeatable processes across the enterprise.

A process map is an amazing tool that generates a number of powerful results, including:

- Showing "who" and "what" is involved in a process and revealing areas where a process is inadequate and requires improvement

- Providing insight into a process to help teams brainstorm ideas for process improvement, increase communication, and provide process documentation

- Identifying bottlenecks, repetition, and delays

- Helping to define process boundaries, process ownership, process responsibilities, and effectiveness measures or process metrics

Despite the fact that the benefits of mapping a company's core processes are virtually endless, it is very rarely employed. In most cases, the lack of process maps can be chalked up to business owners believing they don't have time to produce them. The fact of the matter is, inexpensive software tools are now readily available online that have totally streamlined the mapping of processes. Employing an effective "80/20" series of process maps—the 20 percent of a process that delivers 80 percent of the value/results—can quickly reduce costs.

The 80/20 rule applies all the way up the organization chart:

- What are the 20 percent of *team* activities that deliver 80 percent of the *team's* value/results?

- What are the 20 percent of *department* activities that deliver 80 percent of the *department's* value/results?

- What are the 20 percent of *function* (i.e., finance, marketing, operations) activities that deliver 80 percent of the *function's* value/results?

    - What are the 20 percent of *company* activities that deliver 80 percent of the *company's* value/results?

Wow! Imagine if your company had the answer to these questions. Imagine if your company had the processes associated with the 80/20 activities clearly mapped, and training was developed based on those maps. A substantial increase in the metrics that will drive a doubling of a company's valuation often begins with the mapping of core processes.

Invest in Automation and Systems

A huge by-product of process-mapping activities is the opportunity to review existing business processes (even if they are just undocumented practices) in an effort to reduce redundancies. Most often these efficiencies are discovered in the production phase. The next step is to determine if automating any of the production processes is a possibility. The implementation of information system and/or the automation of a production process may significantly decrease the cost of producing units as more are ordered, and significantly increase the scalability of the business model.

Eventually, that Excel spreadsheet your company uses to track customers is going to be unwieldy, and manually creating financial reports isn't going to cut it. Online software applications like customer-relationship management, order management, time tracking, and financial-reporting systems and protocols provide platforms to automate routine tasks, capture information, and prevent duplication of effort. The resulting advantage is that everyone has access to the best information for satisfying the needs of the customer. All of this can be realized without the additional head count that is normally associated with revenue growth.

So automate to the max! A business that is labor intensive and staff intensive is not scalable. The best advice is to start early by looking at production automation, proven process technologies, and minimum staff approaches, before you begin scaling. Document processes and build online training videos so new people can come online quickly and consistently.

A final note on automation and systems: The prospect of implementing software can be extremely intimidating for a lower mid-tier company. The magic of fractional resources is that you can bring in a fractional CTO (Chief Technology Officer) who can pull together a needs assessment, identify the best technology, and assess the best-in-class vendor(s) for the technology. They can also manage the implementation of the software as an IT project, in order to make certain your company experiences the returns you are looking for.

Reduce Delivery Times

In order to find scalable aspects in our clients' business models, we first locate the aspects of their business that can be replicated quickly and cost effectively. If the next sale requires just as much time and effort as the one prior to it, then the business model is not scalable. In the case of software companies, once the costly development stage is complete, the company can sell as many copies of the software as it wants, as fast as it needs to, with very little incremental cost. This is the very epitome of scalability. We encourage our clients to think about how the delivery of their product could be automated in a way that would allow them to produce the product faster and cheaper for every additional customer who buys it.

Consider how Expedia.com changed the entire travel industry. Since the dawn of time (and flights), travelers had to choose between handling their own travel arrangements or seeking a travel agent. Both ways yielded a slow, inefficient process because an agent can only service one person at a time. When Expedia.com came onto the scene, the entire reservation process was revolutionized. Customers could easily and quickly create travel arrangements without having to pay travel-agent fees. Expedia.com found a way to service one customer with the same ease as servicing 1 million customers.

Companies that can automate the delivery process of their goods or services are easily scalable. How is your product delivered? How can you automate it? Once you have determined that, you've found an area of scalability in your business.

Manage Working Capital

How a company expects to make money is an important part of its business model. The timeliness of the cash receipts is another important factor. As depicted in the "Working Capital Cycle" graphic, some companies run up costs (raw materials, inventory) and spend cash (sales activities) months before any cash is collected.

The funds required to bridge this period are commonly referred to as working capital, and it is a very important concept to understand.

Many, if not most, business owners are confused by working capital. This is a huge issue because the lack of access to adequate working capital and financing options is a predominant factor in a business failing to grow.

Although inadequate access to working capital manifests itself in chronic cash shortages, working capital does not equal cash. The definition of working capital is the difference between current assets (cash, accounts receivable, etc.) and current liabilities (accounts payable, accrued expenses, etc.). Based on this definition, it is clear that cash is only a part of the equation.

The easiest way to explain working capital is the difference (measured in number of days) between when a company pays for things and when it gets paid. Here is a simplified example:

1. Cash goes out to pay for parts and labor to build a product.
2. After ten days the product is ready to be sold.
3. It takes another twenty days to sell the product to a customer on credit (net-thirty terms).
4. If the customer pays on time, the working capital cycle is sixty days.

The company needs to have enough "working capital" to fund this transaction until it gets paid. This may not have been a problem at twenty people, but it becomes a huge problem at 50–60 people. To begin with, the immediate funding requirements for weekly/monthly payroll are going to double or triple!

Working-capital shortages precipitate a need to "rent" money. A company's need to rent money may increase its cost by more than 2 percent of revenues. In our scaling example at the beginning of this chapter, the goal was to increase EBITDA by an additional 5 percent. In some instances, we could achieve 20–40 percent of our goal by simply decreasing the need to finance operations with rented money.

It should also be noted that a company constrained by a lack of working capital tends to have an additional list of simmering issues that become major financial problems as a company attempts to scale:

- Not having timely and actionable financial statements
- Not controlling costs, particularly personnel expenses
- A focus on revenue instead of profitability, therefore not paying attention to the margin of jobs or sales
- Not anticipating needed growth capital
- Not saving during good times, so that you have a fund for tough times.
- Not refining your business model to stay competitive and meet the emerging needs of your customers
- Ineffective marketing

All of these problems have to be addressed in order to de-risk the company in the eyes of a potential buyer. And, in many companies, these problems prevent the enterprise from obtaining a reasonable interest rate on rented money, if they are able to obtain a working-capital line of credit at all.

Embracing Change

Scaling well requires change. Although it sounds counterintuitive, the products, services, and business model that led to a company's original growth may need to change as the company continues to grow. The company may need to reduce the number of products it offers to focus on those that sell best. Alternatively, it may need to look at line extensions that break into markets the company hasn't served before. Being resistant to change makes an organization stagnant and susceptible to missing important opportunities.

Develop a Plan and Execute It

The *Scaling to Exit* program will create a great exit plan for the client company. The consulting team, in collaboration with the business owner and his/her team, masterfully execute that great plan. It is the job of the corporate development resource to make certain that this is the case; to make certain that the project remains "In the Zone"—as defined in the following graphic:

* *Failure to Launch*—occurs when a company has a great plan but executes it poorly

- *Latent Capacity*—occurs when a company has great execution with a poor plan, or without a plan at all

- *Trouble Spot*—occurs when a company has a poor plan, or no plan at all, and as a result executes poorly or does not execute at all

- *In the Zone*—occurs when a company has a great plan and masterfully executes that great plan

Most companies are squarely in the "Latent Capacity" quadrant. They execute well but do a really poor job of planning. One of the major impediments to effective planning is breaking the tyranny of the urgent and important.

In a 1954 speech to the Second Assembly of the World Council of Churches, former U.S. President Dwight D. Eisenhower, in quoting a colleague, said, "I have two kinds of problems: the urgent and the important. The urgent are not important, and the important are never urgent." This "Eisenhower Principle" is said to be how he organized his workload and priorities.

Most people—entrepreneurial CEOs included—spend the majority of their time at work in the "urgent and important" quadrant. While spending time there is definitely better than spending time in the "not urgent and not important" quadrant, it is not the ideal place to be. The ideal quadrant is the "important but not urgent" quadrant. This is the quadrant where the magic happens.

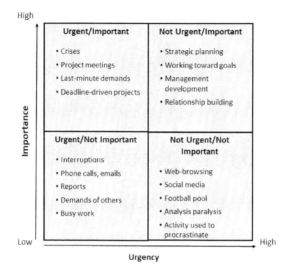

Visioning, strategic planning, developing goals to achieve critical success factors, and developing and executing the action plans necessary to achieve those goals are all very *important* activities. By their very nature, however, they are not *urgent*.

People typically spend a lot of time on "urgent and important" activities. As a result, they have no time left for the "important but not urgent" activities that will actually move their company forward. This is why so many business owners feel overwhelmed. Instead of having a mature ten-year-old company, they have a company that has been in business one year, ten times over. There is a world of difference between the two. A company that doesn't set goals (big, aggressive goals) is at best operating in the "urgent and important" quadrant. At worst the company is vacillating between "urgent but not important" or "not urgent and not important."

When company executives spend too much time on "urgent and important" activities, the negative impact to the company is always significant. Inevitably the leaders of these companies end up operating at two or three levels below where they should be, and it means that there is no one sitting in the driver's seat. There is no vision, and there is no strategy—in the words of Dave Mason, "There is just you and me and we both disagree."

You Have Got to Want It

Awhile back, a colleague introduced me to a middle-aged owner of a fairly successful Parisian bakery. The business had fourteen employees and generated a little more than $1.25 million in annual sales. The revenues were generated through walk-in customers at a retail store and through a wholesale business with local grocery stores. This baker had recently been invited to become a provider in the *Amazon Fresh* program and was therefore sitting on a huge growth opportunity—one that called for a four-fold increase in the capacity of the business.

When I explained what would be involved in scaling the company to take on this meteoric growth, the owners ultimately decided that they were more comfortable remaining a small company than scaling to a large enterprise. The irony is that the changes required to become a large enterprise are the same changes that would enable them to experience really profitable growth as a small company. In three to five years, the company would be worth at least five times more than it is worth today. Without those changes, in three to five years the company will be right where it is now.

This story will resonate for many. I have several more like it. The lesson to be learned is that if you have a vision for doubling your valuation, you will need to have an appetite for designing and executing a plan. If you don't know where you are going, any road will get you there. To paraphrase an exchange in Lewis Carroll's *Alice's Adventures in Wonderland*:

Alice: Would you tell me, please, which way I ought to go from here?

The Cheshire Cat: That depends a good deal on where you want to get to.

Three

Scaling Management

Scaling the business model to scale EBITDA is a big piece of the doubling-valuation puzzle, but it is not the only piece. Scaling a company's management is also important, because management is one of the primary levers that increases the attractiveness of the enterprise to outside buyers.

Many lower mid-tier companies are a reflection of their owners. Unfortunately, when the owner *is* the business, and he/she leaves, there is a high likelihood the business will fall apart. A business is probably ready to go to market when the owner can be out for at least a month and his/her absence does not hurt cash flow. A really effective strategy for making sure the company is sustainable without the owner's constant presence begins with establishing a compelling vision that is bigger than the owner.

Establishing a Compelling Vision

As previously noted, the "True North" of the organization alignment model is the *Vision*. It is the responsibility of leadership to clearly articulate a compelling vision for the organization.

So much has been written about the importance of having a compelling vision that many executives have become desensitized to it. Yet the very definition of a leader is one who articulates a vision of the future that is so compelling that others follow it despite their current circumstances.

Maximizing the valuation of your company really is all about articulating a compelling vision—a vision for your future and the future of your company. It is a non-negotiable, and it is singularly the purview of leadership. In fact, the absence of a compelling vision is the most obvious indicator of a lack of organizational leadership.

The following graphic clearly communicates two facts:

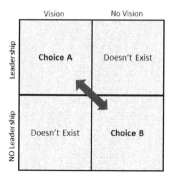

(1) Vision cannot exist when [effective] leadership is not present; and, (2) [effective] leadership doesn't exist when there is a lack of vision.

As a business owner, the only two choices you are left with are: (1) have [effective] leaders who are articulating a compelling vision; or, (2) abdicate [effective] leadership by not articulating a compelling vision.

When you think about it that way, there is really only one choice.

The Business Owner as the Road Block

Building a strong team requires the business owner to take him/herself out of the critical path. If the owner is still spending most of his/her time working "in" the business, rather than "on" the business, then he/she is not yet ready to scale. Most business owners that we have worked with admit to being overwhelmed by the breadth of issues they are confronted with as they experience growth in the lower mid-tier. It is not unusual for a business owner's day to begin at 7 AM with a discussion on a new product and include a meeting at 10 AM on a human-resources issue and a meeting at 1 PM on a legal issue. If this describes your day, then you, in all likelihood, are in the critical path.

It's impossible for anyone to be an expert in all aspects of the business, and yet the business owner assumes that he/she must accept the task of making every important decision. As a company grows it becomes more and more difficult for the business owner to make the right decisions. The following matrix provides a very simple and helpful illustration.

Stage 1—*unconscious incompetence*:	The stage in which you aren't aware of what you don't know about a particular subject
Stage 2—*conscious incompetence*:	The stage in which you become aware of what you don't know about a particular subject

| Stage 3—*conscious competence*: | The stage in which you are aware that you know things that you previously didn't know about a particular subject |
| Stage 4—*unconscious competence*: | The stage in which you become unaware of all that you know about a particular subject |

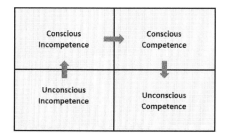

The ideal management team is composed of an owner and 3–4 people who each have achieved "*unconscious competence*" in a particular major functional area (i.e., operations, finance, sales & marketing).

This of course is extremely rare. It is more often the case that the management team for a lower mid-tier company is comprised of a business owner and 2–3 dedicated people who are trying to keep the wheels on the bus.

Perhaps the most common conceptualization of the matrix is that the owner (and the company's investors and employees) wrongly assumes him/herself to be at stage 2— "*conscious incompetence*" (the owner knows what he/she doesn't know)—and is working towards achieving stage 3:

1. The business owner is aware of all the skill(s) required to profitably grow the company.

2. The business owner is aware that he/she don't possess all the skill(s).

3. The business owner will recognize the benefits to be afforded from acquiring all the skill(s).

In reality, outside of a specific area of expertise, the majority of lower mid-tier business owners are really at stage 1 (i.e., they don't know what they don't know). When the business owner is at stage 1, none of the important acknowledgments are taking place, and no one can hope to achieve *"conscious competence"* until they've become consciously aware of their own incompetence. This is a fundamental reason a lot of companies fail to grow.

When a business owner makes a bad decision, the impact on the organization goes well beyond the financial. Employees become frustrated because they want their leaders to provide clarity of purpose and performance expectations and to chart a roadmap for the future. They expect leadership from their leaders. Instead, many employees in lower mid-tier companies are led by business owners who lack vision and mismanage scarce corporate resources. This contributes mightily to the private-equity perception that most companies are not well run. It also explains why so few companies are successfully sold.

Buyers Wants a Strong Management Team

All of the unflattering generalizations of the business owner notwithstanding, these individuals have developed and maintained sizable companies that employ nearly one-half of the US workforce! They are doing something right. So once the owner leaves, the remaining management team will have to serve as the backbone of the company while the new owners assess the needs of the business. As most investors prefer a cohesive and competent management unit to be in place before putting their dollars in, most offers come with high expectations for an existing management team. The importance of an experienced and skilled management team cannot be underscored enough.

We have about three years to double your valuation and make your company attractive to a buyer. That means that we have about three years to build a strong management team at your firm. The first step is to take stock of your existing management team, paying particular attention to their mindsets and leadership attributes, as these will be invaluable to the sale process. When evaluating the management team of a prospective business, investors will almost certainly look for a cohesive collection of managers. Why? Because change can be tumultuous, especially at the top, and employees will seek a steadying and assertive presence from the existing management team post-sale.

The following questions identify some of the most important things you must consider when determining the value of your management team:

- How active are you, as the owner, on a day-to-day basis?

- Who do key customers call when there is a problem?

- Do key managers receive performance reviews, and are they performing to expectations?

- Do key management employees think and act like owners?

- If you, the owner, were hit by the proverbial "bus", how would the company operate?

- Does the management team meet as a group to discuss short- and long-term strategic goals with the owner?

Rest assured that a private equity buyer will critically assess the value that your management team contributes to your business. We have seen attractive offers erode in value after operational due diligence reveals that the management team is not strong enough to maintain or increase the profitability of the business. Therefore, it's important for owners to mentor and develop the right team members into management roles. These team members must be capable of providing operational detail and answers when needed and of articulating or demonstrating their competency and value when called upon.

As an owner seeking to exit in the next 3–5 years, you should continually assess the strengths and weaknesses of your management team. The sooner you begin evaluating your management team, the more options you will have to ensure that the team will be desirable and valuable to the buyer.

The Secret Weapon—Frontline Managers

Harvey MacKay authored a book entitled *Dig Your Well Before You're Thirsty*. The gist of the book is that you have to build a network long before you need a network. If you wait until you need a network before you begin to build one, it's too late.

In the same vein, you need to develop your management team long before you need your management team to stand on its own. If you wait until you need your managers to stand on their own before you begin to develop them, it is too late.

Unfortunately, the task of growing managers—first to manage and then to lead—is one of the hardest before us. In the compressed 3–5 year timeframe, decisions to either promote existing employees into key management positions or to bring in people in from outside become extremely critical. For business owners who decide to promote existing employees, skill development becomes essential. For business owners who decide to look outside of the organization for managers, being an attractive and competitive workplace becomes essential.

If the strength of the management team will make or break a deal with a private equity buyer, and it is extremely difficult and time consuming to develop a strong management team, what should you do? Well, you start at the top. You, as the business owner, must be willing to become aware of your *unconscious incompetence*, and be open to closing those gaps. Then you must go to work on your senior managers and your frontline managers.

This emphasis on developing frontline managers is the radical component of the Scaling to Exit program. We focus on developing frontline managers because scaling is all about growing revenues at a rate greater than the corresponding expense. In other words, if we experience a year-over-year increase in sales, and we are able to deliver on those increased sales with our existing workforce, then we will increase our EBITDA on a year-over-year basis. We will scale the company and substantially increase its valuation. Only the frontline managers can make this happen.

The Brandon Hall Group's 2016–2017 Training Benchmarking Study reveals a paradox that has existed since the early 1950s.

- 58 percent of companies spent more than $1,000 per learner per year for senior-level managers
- 32 percent of companies spent more than $1,000 per learner per year for mid-level managers
- 23 percent of companies spent more than $1,000 per learner per year for frontline managers
- 39 percent of companies spent more than $1,000 per learner per year for high potential employees
- 17 percent of companies spent more than $1,000 per leaner per year for individual contributors

The paradox is that frontline managers are responsible for the day-to-day productivity of the workforce—the single largest expense item on the income statement—but they receive less than half of the training that senior managers receive. It would seem that it would be the other way around, but in a book entitled *The Leadership Pipeline*, Ram Charan and his co-authors explain why it is not.

In the book, the authors uncover a vicious cycle. In most companies, individual contributors get promoted to frontline-manager roles because of the great work they have done as individual contributors. Rather than allow them to acquire and develop much-needed managerial skills, the mid-level manager will expect the frontline manager to "figure it out" while continuing to produce as an individual contributor. The frontline manager quickly learns that frontline management means producing work product and, when absolutely necessary, addressing a supervisory issue. It becomes apparent to them that "tending to the caring and feeding" of employees is not valued in their company.

The vicious cycle occurs when the frontline managers in these companies are promoted to mid-level manager positions. They pass along to their new frontline managers the "don't tend to the caring and feeding of employees" organizational trait, and the cycle starts again. By the time someone in this organization gets promoted to a senior leadership position, this trait has been embedded into the organizational culture. The only way to break the cycle is for the business owner to begin to value the skills associated with "tending to the caring and feeding" of employees—frontline management skills. When the vicious cycle becomes a virtuous one, the organizational culture can begin to improve.

About the Workforce

Here is the reality. Most industries are in a war for talent.

The US Department of Labor tells us that labor-force churn—the number of people who leave jobs and start new jobs—is rising. Generally speaking, more churn signals a healthier labor market.

Aging Baby Boomers are exiting the workforce as they reach retirement age, and companies locally and nationally are scrambling to keep their valuable institutional knowledge from leaving with them. Virtually every industry has a name for the phenomena, including, "The Big Crew Change" in oil and gas, and the "Silver Tsunami" in government.

The numbers are eye popping: AARP, the non-profit advocacy group for Americans age fifty and older, has said that every day, ten thousand Boomers reach the traditional retirement age of sixty-five. That trend began in 2011 and will continue for the next fourteen years. And as companies try to ensure key business processes are passed to younger employees, they're also dealing with the trend of Millennials changing jobs with greater frequency than previous generations—and taking their newly inherited knowledge with them.

According to Deloitte and the Manufacturing Institute, over the next decade, nearly 3.5 million manufacturing jobs will need to be filled. Two million jobs are expected to go unfilled due to the skills gap. Moreover, a similar report indicates that 80 percent of manufacturers report a moderate or serious shortage of qualified applicants for skilled and highly skilled production positions.

Labor-force churn, Baby Boomer exits, and the Millennial propensity to change jobs, places a tremendous amount of pressure on the remaining workforce to be as productive as possible. The last element to complete the "perfect storm" is the fact that—according to Gallup—70 percent of the workforce is not engaged and therefore not productive. In the foreseeable future, all indicators point to a very tight, transient, and fluid workforce. Truly it has become easier to find a new customer than to find a good employee. How does a company get any leverage out of its workforce in this environment?

The answer is good managers—specifically, good frontline managers. According to Gallup, only 14 percent of the population will naturally become good frontline managers. The remaining 86 percent of the population can only become a good frontline manager if they receive training and development. Unfortunately, only 10 percent of new managers actually receive training and development. You get the picture. It explains why most people surveyed state that they have never experienced the joy of having a good manager!

Frontline managers need basic "blocking and tackling" skills, such as:

- Active listening
- Giving and receiving feedback
- Problem solving
- Decision making
- Performance management
- Coaching
- Delegating
- Managing teams
- Planning
- Time management

More often than not, frontline managers are not receiving this kind of training. They become frustrated because they have not been equipped to be successful in their roles. As a result, the percentage of engaged managers is only somewhat higher than the percentage of engaged employees. In fact Gallup research found that 65 percent of managers are not engaged.

Predictably, a manager's level of engagement has a direct impact on the engagement level of his/her employees. If 65 percent of [frontline] managers are not engaged, then the odds are pretty high that at least 70 percent of the workforce will not be engaged. The fulcrum point for engagement then is the frontline manager. This is where an increase in engagement can be leveraged the most. There

have been many books written on the subject that
substantiate this claim, but there are three factors that make
the financial impact of trained and engaged frontline
managers real for you the business owner:

1. Employee retention

Decades of Gallup research has verified the fact that
employees don't leave companies, they leave managers.
Improve the quality of your frontline managers, and
increase employee retention.

The cost of employee turnover can be devastating.

For example, if you have a 150-person company with
11 percent annual turnover, and you spend $25,000 per
person on hiring; $10,000 on each for turnover and
development; and experience $50,000 of opportunity
cost in lost productivity on average when refilling each
role, then your annual cost of turnover would be about
$1.4 million.

$$150 \text{ x } 11\% = 16.5 \text{ employees}$$
$$\$25K + \$10K + \$50K = \$85K$$
$$16.5 \text{ x } \$85K = \$1.4M$$

Wow! Assuming an EBITDA of 10 percent, your entire
first $14 million of revenue would go towards covering
the $1.4 million in annual turnover cost. To add insult
to injury, with most industries in the midst of a war for
talent, many companies can't find a timely, qualified
replacement for the turned over resource.

2. Employee Engagement

Engaged employees are productive employees. Having
a trained and engaged frontline manager is highly
correlated to having engaged employees. Obviously

employee productivity is important to any business. The more productive your employees are, the more successful your company will be. There is an abundance of data to corroborate this fact:

- Companies that increase their number of talented managers and double the rate of engaged employees achieve, on average, 147 percent higher earnings per share than their competition.

- 58 percent of employees say poor management is the biggest thing getting in the way of productivity.

- Employees who exercise their strengths on a daily basis are 8 percent more productive and six times more likely to be engaged.

- Teams with high employee-engagement rates are 21 percent more productive and have 28 percent less internal theft than those with low engagement.

- Companies with engaged employees outperform those without by 202 percent.

- High-performing employees have three things in common: talent, high engagement, and ten or more years of service within the company.

- Employees who are engaged are 27 percent more likely to report "excellent" performance.

- 57 percent of employees who said they were very stressed at work felt less productive and disengaged, while only 10 percent of low-stress employees reported feeling this way.

- Organizations with highly engaged employees had an average three-year revenue growth 2.3 times greater than companies whose employees were only engaged at an average level.

- Increasing employee engagement investments by 10 percent can increase profits by $2,400 per employee per year.

- Disengaged workers had 37 percent higher absenteeism, 49 percent more accidents, and 60 percent more errors and defects.

- Organizations with low employee-engagement scores saw 18 percent lower productivity, 16 percent lower profitability, 37 percent lower job growth, and 65 percent lower share price over time.

- Actively disengaged employees cost the U.S. $450 to $550 billion per year in lost productivity.

- Health-care costs at companies where there is a lot of work pressure are almost 50 percent higher than at other organizations.

3. Customer Satisfaction and Retention

Customer satisfaction and retention rates are the highest when employee engagement levels are high. According to a Cvent study, customer retention rates are 18 percent higher when employees are highly engaged.

The question becomes how much does it cost your company to secure a new customer? A $15 million manufacturer that spends an industry average 8 percent of its operating budget ($480,000) on sales and marketing to secure ten new customers per year experiences a customer-acquisition cost of approximately $48,000 per customer.

$$\frac{\text{Total Cost of Sales and Marketing}}{\text{Number of Customers Acquired}} = \text{Average Acquisition Cost per Customer}$$

This equation does not take into account the foregone revenue associated with the customer who has turned over. That number could be 4–5 times higher. Engaged employees could save this sample company hundreds of thousands of dollars each year.

An Equation

Good Managers X *the Scaling to Exit* program = Scalable Growth

The above equation highlights the critical role that "good managers" play in the pursuit of scalable growth. Note that the equation is a multiplication equation versus an addition equation. This is because if the value of either factor approaches zero, then the product will approach zero.

We are so confident in the efficacy of the Scaling to Exit program that we base our brand promise on the fact that it will at least double the valuation of a client company. When we ask our clients to assign a value to the program on a scale from one to ten, they are always very comfortable with assigning it at a rating of nine, at a minimum.

Let's put some numbers to the equation:

Good Managers X *the Scaling to Exit* program = Scalable Growth

$$3 \times 9 = 27$$

Where, on a scale from one to ten, we assign the quality of managers a "3" and the quality and efficacy of the Scaling to Exit program a "9," the output in terms of scalable growth is a 27 points out of a possible 100.

The upside for scalable growth at a client company that further maximizes the impact of the program is minimal:

$$3 \times \underline{10} = 30$$

The upside for scalable growth at a client company that invests in developing their managers is staggering:

$$\underline{7} \times 9 = 63$$

There is no contest. The upside for scalable growth by investing in managers versus attempting to wring more benefit out of the *Scaling to Exit* program is enormous. This upside is realized through an inevitable increase in workforce productivity, employee retention, client satisfaction, and client retention. The equation reveals that the impact of the program will be minimized unless there is a significant investment in frontline manager development.

Be Strategic about Closing Gaps

In the [highly likely] event that we identify a skill gap on the existing management team of a client company, we provide advice and counsel on hiring to meet that need, and the impact that it may have on the ultimate sale price. For example, a client was made aware that any private equity buyer would likely decide that the company needed both a more experienced CFO, and an outside sales representative. Since every dollar used to hire management team talent reduces EBITDA (profitability), spending $250,000 on such positions could possibly result in a $1,500,000 reduction in the sale price (in this case the company ultimately sold for 6X EBITDA, so 6 x $250,000 = $1,500,000).

The client realized that by hiring an outside sales rep with established relationships, he was more likely to generate greater profitability faster than the marginal gains that would be generated by hiring a CFO to replace the currently competent controller. The client did not spend the money to hire the CFO, which resulted in greater profitability and a greater sales price.

Conclusion

One of the most difficult parts of scaling for business owners has to do with their people. It is relatively easy to let go of processes that no longer help the business or tasks that are no longer appropriate. To let go of people requires of company leaders a special will and determination to grow and survive. This is particularly true since most entrepreneurs who successfully start and grow businesses care deeply about their people.

For the business owner who finds him/herself in a situation where some current employees cannot take the business to the next level, there will be a need for honest conversations. Having a conversation with each employee about the needs of the growing business and how management sees his/her future role is essential to keeping employee expectations in line with reality. It is important to tell these employees early on that, as the business scales, there may be the need to bring in some heavy-hitters. Let them know that this means they may be layered. These are not easy conversations, but they are absolutely necessary for the business owner who wants to treat people fairly.

Sometimes scaling the management team comes down to a "make-versus-buy decision." Would it be expedient for the company to grow and scale by thrusting existing people into new roles as the business expands and changes? Or will the business owner have to look outside the organization for the skills, talent, and experience needed to take the company to the next level? Can you, the business owner, remove emotional roadblocks and look at the situation pragmatically?

The fact is, to successfully grow, the owner will have to let go. And sometimes that means letting go of good people who simply cannot grow with the organization. The business owner should also be a good steward of the capable employees who will remain after the sale transaction. Leading up to a sale, make certain you are setting employees up for success by giving them the training, development, coaching, mentoring, and hands-on experience they will need to be considered valuable to the buyer.

Whether you're selling your business, merging, or retiring, effective leadership can make the difference between success and failure. Your business plan should outline the chain of command after you leave and the basics of company decision-making. When a longtime business owner or leader leaves, some companies experience chaos. The chaos typically manifests itself in the form of numerous people fighting over power and forgetting the original goals of the business. By establishing a clear succession plan, you can minimize these risks and keep your company successful for the long term.

Four

Scaling Marketing

For the Baby Boomer business owner seeking to exit his/her company in the next three years, and seeking to at least double the valuation of the company in the interim, scaling the business model for EBITDA growth is a preferred strategy over hyper-revenue growth. But the "holy grail" for doubling EBITDA would be effective scaling combined with hyper-revenue growth. Imagine what the valuation of our hypothetical $20 million manufacturer would be if we managed to double top-line revenue and increase EBITDA by 5 percent at the same time. Instead of doubling their valuation, we would triple it!

Preliminary		Exit	
Revenue	20,000,000	Revenue	40,000,000
EBITDA @ 10%	2,000,000	EBITDA @ 15%	6,000,000
4.5 multiple	9,000,000	4.5 multiple	27,000,000

Marketing Is Hugely Important

The purpose of marketing is to drive a large volume of prospects into a company's sales funnel. At the bottom of the funnel are the leads that a company expects to become customers. Yet, so many lower mid-tier companies fail to set aside a modest percentage of their operating budgets to fund marketing activities. Every company is in the business of generating customers and revenue, although many bypass marketing as one of the most effective means for achieving that end.

Today's marketplace is more complex than it was fifteen years ago. As a result, many Baby Boomer business owners get overwhelmed by marketing and therefore decide to opt out. There have been, and will continue to be, dramatic changes in the world of marketing and advertising. The thing to keep in mind is the fact that the primary purpose of marketing will always stay the same: to build brand awareness; to engage the target audience; to drive traffic, leads, and sales; and to prove industry expertise.

Build Brand Awareness

In order for a company to effectively market its product or service, it must have a clear understanding of its value proposition, and it must know who the ideal consumer of the value proposition is. In other words, it must establish a clear brand. If the company doesn't have a clear, definitive idea of its value proposition, then it certainly can't expect its targeted consumers to understand it.

One of the first activities that the Scaling to Exit fractional Chief Marketing Officer (CMO) engages in is the confirmation and/or development of the client company's value proposition, closely followed by a description of the target customer of that value proposition. To successfully create, or even re-create a strong, successful brand that reaches the target audience, we require our client companies to collaborate internally on the following items:

- Who are we as a company?
- What keywords do people search to find our products/service?
- Who are our buyer personas?
- What makes us different?
- How do we convey our expertise through content and graphics?
- What value are we providing?

- What makes customers buy from us? What makes them return?

Once we have clearly established a foundation for a brand, we can begin executing a marketing campaign to raise brand awareness.

Engage the Target Audience

The fact that your consumers and target audience have the ability to connect and engage in conversations with you (or your competitors) makes it critically important that you're tapping into this potent resource. By staying engaged with your target audience through a variety of marketing tools, you effectively humanize your brand and set yourself up as an ideal organization to buy from or do business with.

Drive Traffic, Leads, and Sales

Over 75 percent of all Internet users conduct product research online. "Getting found" has required a shift from strictly physical advertising to a blend with web-based marketing. The foundation for lead generation in the digital age is quality marketing content delivered on a consistent basis. This means that blogging, eBooks, whitepapers, webinars, podcasts, videos, case studies, and visual content like infographics have become the new standard for generating sufficient traffic to a company's website. The main purpose of this content is to get found in the search engines by customers who are searching relevant terms.

Prove Industry Expertise

As more Millennials take on senior procurement roles in companies, proving industry expertise will become an increasingly important by-product of any successful marketing campaign. Millennials will perform an exhaustive search on a potential product/service provider well in advance of any buy decision, so a company's content, blog articles, offers, client communications, and social media should focus on establishing the company as an industry thought leader. When it comes time for Millennials to open the wallet, this is whom they will look to.

Inbound and Outbound Marketing

Generating high-quality leads and expanding target accounts in a way that generates more sales-ready opportunities is challenging. To take on this challenge, the *Scaling to Exit* fractional CMO will leverage an integrated approach that includes both traditional outbound marketing and web-based inbound marketing.

Outbound marketing refers to any kind of marketing where a company initiates the conversation and sends its message to an audience. Outbound marketing includes traditional forms of marketing and advertising, such as TV commercials, radio ads, print advertisements (newspaper ads, magazine ads, flyers, brochures, catalogs, etc.), tradeshows, outbound sales calls (or "cold calls"), and email.

Inbound marketing is the opposite of outbound marketing. With inbound marketing, the customers find you when they need you. Examples of inbound marketing include content marketing, blogging, SEO, and opt-in email marketing. Paid search advertising is considered inbound marketing because a company's ads only appear when people are searching for products or services that the company offers.

Striking a balance between inbound and outbound marketing enables a company to settle on the most successful strategies to capture leads and move prospects through its sales cycle. In the *Scaling to Exit* program, we ask client companies to employ three best-practice strategies:

1. Commit To and Budget For an Integrated Marketing Program

Sixty to seventy percent of the sales cycle is finished before a prospect reaches a sales person. Potential customers are researching solutions, and companies must leverage inbound marketing to be online and in the places where potential customers are in order to become a part of the considered set. It takes 7–16 touches to move a target prospect through the sales funnel. Outbound marketing allows the company to provide valuable educational content in an integrated and strategic fashion to move prospects along the buyer's journey. Budgeting for both methods ensures the greatest opportunity for success in filling the sales pipeline.

2. Map Inbound and Outbound Content and Touches to the Buyer's Journey

Taking the time to research and set up personas for key industries and documenting their inbound and outbound journeys will help a company map the experience funnel for prospects.

3. Use Inbound Data to Inform the Outbound Efforts

Inbound efforts will bring prospects into the top of the funnel, but it can be difficult to tell which of these prospects is genuinely interested in a company's product or service. This is where data comes in. By digging through social profiles (using one of many social-selling tools available) of inbound leads, the company can determine the best ones to focus their outbound efforts on.

The ideal marketing strategy recognizes the strengths and weaknesses in both marketing directions and thoughtfully combines them into a cohesive message with a comprehensive reach. Inbound and outbound marketing should be considered teammates, not competitors.

Manufacturing—A Sample Case Study for Marketing Effectiveness

I was very intrigued by a flood of data that suggested that inbound marketing has been extremely effective for the manufacturing industry. I decided to look into it a little further. My research yielded the ideal buyer persona for the *Scaling to Exit* value proposition.

Buyer personas (sometimes referred to as marketing personas) are fictional, generalized representations of the ideal customer for a company. Personas help the marketing, sales, and products and services departments internalize the ideal customers, and relate to those customers as real humans. Having a deep understanding of the company's buyer persona(s) is critical to driving content creation, product development, sales follow-up, and anything that relates to customer acquisition and retention.

The five reasons why manufacturers (and other similar industries) are great candidates for inbound marketing are the same five reasons that manufacturers are great candidates for the *Scaling to Exit* program.

1. Manufacturing Businesses Are Mature

Whether the manufacturers are producing labels, welding equipment, safety products, or rail systems, most of these businesses have been around for a long time. They're successful businesses looking for ways to keep up with changing buyer behavior. They've seen a slow and steady degrading of the marketing tactics they used historically and now are looking for more innovative approaches to marketing and sales.

They're not changing their businesses, but they are interested in telling their story differently. They are providing more self-service information to prospects in active sales cycles and taking a more proactive, data-driven approach to sales and marketing.

Because their businesses are mature, there's a lot of certainty around whom they're selling to, what pains those people have, and how steadfast businesses solve their challenges. After all, in some cases, these businesses have been doing just that for hundreds of years.

For our client companies, we adapt their future sales and marketing strategy to fit their existing businesses. They have the success stories required to help their prospects feel safe; we simply repackage that content and deliver it in a way that matches today's buyers. More electronic conversations, better website experiences, ongoing lead nurturing, and new educational content all produce results for these businesses.

2. Leadership Is Patient

Manufacturing companies tend to have a consistent approach to leadership. They're patient. They understand that good marketing takes time. Perhaps because they're used to making big investments in machinery that takes years to pay off, or perhaps because they have to manage those assets effectively to ensure they produce gains, manufacturers look at marketing with a long-term perspective.

Inbound requires (actually demands) this long-term perspective. A company can't try inbound marketing for a few months to see if it works. A company can't try inbound marketing at a starter level of investment to see if it works. A company can't try inbound marketing by paying partial attention to it while it does three or four other things at the same time. With inbound marketing, a company should either go all-in or not at all.

In my conversations with the leaders of manufacturing companies along the front range of Colorado, it is apparent that they use long-term thinking when it comes to their attempts to innovate marketing and sales at their companies.

3. They Follow the Guidance of Trusted Advisors

A lot of the manufacturing company leaders I've spoken with are very comfortable identifying areas of their business where they are not experts. In those areas, they are not hesitant to bring in smart people and follow their advice. They view these people as partners.

In other industries we have worked in, this is not necessarily the case. Oftentimes consultants are viewed as vendors who have been engaged to simply do a job. That perspective opens the door for a lot of second-guessing, wasted cycles, and slower-to-perform programs. For companies that want to add an inbound channel, the fastest way to do so is to hire someone who has done it hundreds of times before and then get out of the way.

4. Manufacturing Companies Streamline Internal Processes

Manufacturers know the value of a streamlined process. Many of them are ISO certified. They know that the more efficient they are, the more money they make. They're sensitive to process and limiting wasted cycles, which aligns nicely with inbound marketing. The fewer wasted cycles, the faster we get to publish assets and adjust and improve performance.

Engagements with manufacturing companies often run smoother and with less rework because leaders trust vendors, and also because leaders know that doing the back-and-forth thing is counterproductive. They engage with us to streamline the production, review, approval, and optimization processes inherent to inbound programs. The result is that our team is able to move through planning faster, produce assets more efficiently, create lead-generating tools earlier in the engagement, and, as a result, produce results sooner. Over time, those results grow faster because of our ability to act quickly.

5. They Invest at Appropriate Levels

This may be attributed to the fact that manufacturers are comfortable with investing in large and expensive machines. It may also be attributed to expectations associated with the ROI from those investments. Or it could simply be that they've been investing appropriately in marketing all along and are just moving towards a better balance of traditional outbound tactics with more inbound tactics. Regardless of the reason, the fact is, manufacturing clients are willing to invest at the appropriate levels to deliver on their business goals.

In most cases, these companies are also not planning to double revenue in twelve months. They're looking for a consistent and regular 10–15 percent growth year over year, and at their sizes (most of these companies are not small) they are aware of the investment required to maintain revenue levels and to grow those levels at reasonable clips.

Investing the right amount in marketing enables a company's internal team, or external agency team, to do everything necessary to grow the business. Contrast that with coming in with a discount plan, and then each month talking about tactics that they would like to do but can't fit into the budget. Companies that have aggressive goals must invest accordingly in marketing.

There are a lot of generalizations here, and many of them are based upon our observations over the years. However, the consistencies are too frequent to be considered pure luck. There are legitimate reasons why these stable, financially responsible, historically successful companies are seeing serious results from their move to inbound marketing.

More significantly, the lessons that may be extracted from these successes will have a dramatic impact on a client company's ability to generate leads, hit their revenue targets, scale their company, and double their valuation.

Marketing Return on Investment (MROI)

Marketing is an essential part of most businesses and can pay many times over what it costs. To make the most of the marketing spend, however, the business owner needs to know how to measure its results. Marketing firms will sometimes try to distract with softer metrics, but MROI (Marketing Return on Investment) is the one that matters for most businesses. The MROI of any marketing campaign ultimately comes in the form of increased sales.

The MROI may be calculated with the following equation:

(Sales Growth - Marketing Cost) / Marketing Cost = MROI

According to Nielsen, the average MROI is $1.09. A $1.09 MROI means that for every $1 spent, the company generates $2.09 (for a profit of $1.09). In percentage terms, this is a 109 percent return on investment (ROI). Nielsen research indicates that the top three marketing media, with the highest average ROI, are email marketing, search-engine optimization, and direct mail.

The CMO Survey, sponsored by the Fuqua School of Business at Duke University, Deloitte LLP, and the American Marketing Association (AMA) provides an additional really important data point for analysis. The CMO Survey found that marketing budgets now comprise 11 percent of total company budgets on average (Figure 1), up slightly from 10.4 percent in February 2012, when the CMO Survey first asked this question.

As indicated by the research, consumer-packaged-goods companies allocate by far the largest percent of total company budget to marketing (nearly one quarter), followed by consumer services, tech software/biotech, communications/media, and mining/construction. Companies that spend the smallest portion of their budgets on marketing include transportation, manufacturing, and energy.

Figure 1: Marketing Budgets By Industry
Marketing accounts for what percentage of your overall budget?

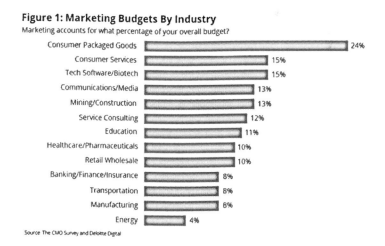

Industry	Percentage
Consumer Packaged Goods	24%
Consumer Services	15%
Tech Software/Biotech	15%
Communications/Media	13%
Mining/Construction	13%
Service Consulting	12%
Education	11%
Healthcare/Pharmaceuticals	10%
Retail Wholesale	10%
Banking/Finance/Insurance	8%
Transportation	8%
Manufacturing	8%
Energy	4%

Source: The CMO Survey and Deloitte Digital

We have the fictitious $15 million company that goes by the name Mile-High Manufacturing (MHM). MHM has the following financial data:

- Revenues of $15 million
- Gross Profits of 50 percent
- EBITDA of 10 percent

Based on this information, we can back into $6 million as an estimate of the operating budget:

Estimated Operating Budget	
Revenue	$15,000,000.00
COGS	$7,500,000.00
Gross Profit	$7,500,000.00
Operating Expenses	**$6,000,000.00**
EBITDA	$1,500,000.00

Now let's assume that the MHM marketing spend is at the industry standard of 8 percent of the operating budget. We could calculate MHM's marketing budget to be $480,000 ($6 million x .08 = $480,000).

With these data points and the equation, we can conclude that MHM must experience $1M in sales growth in order for them to achieve Nielsen's 1.09 average MROI:

(Sales Growth - Marketing Cost) / Marketing Cost = MROI

($1,005,000 - $480,000) / $480,000 = MROI

$525,000 / $480,000 = MROI

1.09 = MROI

If you think that this MROI method is too confusing, Chris Leone of *WebStrategies* offered an alternative in a 2016 *WebStrategies* blog. According to Leone, calculating marketing ROI the "traditional" way isn't always practical because calculating MROI manually for each marketing campaign takes time and access to company financials. The approach also requires incredible patience. It could be months before knowing if a campaign was profitable.

Leone proposed that we shelve the complex formulas and algorithms and focus on one simple metric: the revenue-to-marketing-cost ratio. This ratio defines how much money is generated for every dollar spent on marketing. For example, five dollars in sales for every one dollar spent on marketing yields a 5:1 ratio of revenue to cost. Leone says a good marketing ROI is 5:1.

In fact, a 5:1 ratio is middle of the bell curve. A ratio over 5:1 is considered strong for most businesses, and a 10:1 ratio is exceptional. Achieving a ratio higher than 10:1 ratio is possible, but it shouldn't be the expectation. A client company's target ratio would be largely dependent on their cost structure and will vary depending on their industry.

The Scaling to Exit Approach

The fact that the average manufacturer has to invest $480,000 in marketing in order to grow revenue by $1 million doesn't sound very appealing. Leone's revenue-to-marketing-cost ratio confirms my suspicions:

Increase in sales/marketing cost = X
$1,005,000/$480,000 = 2.09

If a ratio of 5:1 is strong, it would seem that a ratio of 2:1 is abysmal.

Leone's revenue-to-marketing-cost ratio is radical. It is easy to understand and easy to apply, but more importantly it is an excellent tool for managing the effectiveness of the marketing spend in the program. Before any marketing activity is started, everyone understands what it needs to generate in order to be successful. With the appropriate tracking mechanisms are in place, everyone can quickly determine if a campaign was successful or not.

When calculating the ratio, we define a marketing cost as any incremental cost incurred to execute that campaign (i.e. the variable costs). These cost include:

- pay-per-click spend
- display-ad clicks
- media spend
- content-production costs
- outside marketing and advertising agency fees

Because full-time marketing personnel costs are fixed, they are not factored into this ratio. The ratio is meant to give campaigns a simple "pass/fail" test, so the costs factored into the ratio should only occur if the campaign runs.

You may ask why 5:1 is a strong ratio. It is because at an absolute minimum, the company must cover the cost of making the product and the cost to market it. A 2:1 revenue-to-marketing-cost ratio wouldn't be profitable for many businesses, as the cost to produce or acquire the item being sold (COGS) is about 50 percent of the sale price. For these businesses, if you spend $100 in marketing to generate $200 in sales, and it costs $100 to make the product being sold, you are breaking even. If all you accomplish with your marketing is break even, you might as well not do it.

Companies with higher gross margins (i.e., their COGS are less than 50 percent of the sales price) may achieve lower sales from their marketing efforts and still remain profitable. Therefore, their ratio is lower. Meanwhile, companies with lower margins (i.e., their COGS is more than 50 percent the sales price) need to stretch their marketing dollars further. Their ratio is higher.

Marketing is all about generating revenue. Marketers who aren't serious about tying their activity to revenues are missing the bigger picture. Implementing a ratio, and treating it as the "golden metric" for marketing activity, will focus the team on the ultimate outcome: scaling the business. Every $1 spent on marketing campaigns should yield approximately $5 in revenue.

Where do your current sales and marketing activities fall on the following scale?

Best Case	Neutral Case	Worst Case
You measure and track the ROI of all your marketing investments.	You calculate ROI on some investments, but because it can get complex, you don't attempt to measure it at all times.	You don't measure the performance of any of your investments.
Your campaigns deliver the highest possible returns and you're able to improve them over time.	You have a general idea of how your investments perform relative to each other, but you can't pinpoint the exact return you're generating.	In fact, marketing is viewed as a cost, not an investment at all.

Your company isn't sure what works and what doesn't, and it's a struggle to meet goals. |
| Your organization understands and agrees with the choices you make because there's solid data to support your investments. | In tough times, you cut the marketing budget. | |

For companies attempting to scale, the best-case scenario is the only acceptable scenario.

Marketing and Sales Organizations

The organization and management of sales and marketing is an important strategic decision that has major repercussions for company growth over time. According to the CMO Survey:

- 67 percent of companies give marketing and sales joint responsibility
- 13 percent do not have a sales function
- 10 percent put sales in charge of marketing

- 7.5 percent put marketing in charge of sales
- 2.5 percent do not have a marketing function

A deeper analysis reveals that marketing spending is higher at companies that give marketing responsibility for sales (17.7 percent of overall budgets) than at firms where sales is responsible for marketing (10.1 percent of budgets). The very nature of marketing is more strategic and customer driven, so it can help ensure that sales activities do not become tactical and short-term. When the sales function sits within marketing, sales can be driven to focus on the acquisition and retention of the most valuable customers for the long run.

Five

Scaling Sales

Generating qualified leads is the biggest challenge for scaling marketing. Converting leads to sales is the biggest challenge for scaling sales.

The purpose of the marketing function is to drive a large volume of prospects into the company's sales funnel. The purpose of the sales function is to convert those prospects into customers as they make their way down the funnel.

For most client companies, an achievable strategy for doubling EBITDA is to generate a 10 percent year-over-year increase in sales while simultaneously decreasing expenses (COGS and/or general & administrative) by 5 percent.

In the *Scaling to Exit* program, we scale sales by targeting the sales experience. We make certain our client companies examine exactly how they perform in this area by asking the following questions:

- What are the most influential drivers of the sales experience?
- What things are the sales reps doing that could damage relationships?
- How does customer perception of the company's sales force compare to the perception of a competitor's sales force?

Companies can begin to identify and pursue the right fixes when they know and understand the answers to these questions.

There are many strategies to grow a company's customer base and increase sales. The strategies and methodologies employed will depend on the business, industry, and region. There are a few best practices that help the sales force target market customers and communicate with them in relevant and meaningful ways.

A recent McKinsey survey was conducted of more than 1,200 purchasing decision-makers in small, medium, and large companies throughout the United States and Western Europe. The survey yielded interesting insights that were consistent across end users and purchasing professionals, regardless of whether the products that they were purchasing were simple or complex.

The primary insight is that there is a big difference between what customers said was important and what actually drove their behavior. Customers insisted price and product aspects were the dominant factors that influenced their opinion of a supplier's performance and, as a result, their purchasing decisions. Yet when the researchers examined what actually determined how a customer rated a vendor's performance, the most important factors were product or service features and the overall sales experience. The upside of getting these two elements right is significant: a primary supplier seen as having a high-performing sales force can boost its share of a customer's business by an average of 8–15 percentage points.

The first insight makes the next finding all the more important. Of the many habits that undermine the sales experience, two that are relatively easy to fix accounted for 55 percent of the behavior customers described as "most destructive": failing to have adequate product knowledge and contacting customers too frequently. Only 3 percent said they weren't contacted enough, suggesting customers are open to fewer, more meaningful interactions. Striking the right balance in customer interaction requires understanding their stated and actual needs.

In the *Scaling to Exit* program, we work with our client companies to make certain there is a clear strategy for reaching out to customers based on needs and profit potential, with schedules dictating frequency. The best contact calendars center around events that create value for customers, such as semiannual business reviews, and which provide an opportunity to assess customer needs and ensure satisfaction. When it comes to building valuable relationships with customers, sales reps are critical players on the front lines. One key is for sales to recognize that customers want to lower their interaction costs, so any contact must be meaningful. Sales reps should also know their products or services intimately and how their offering compares to those of their competitors. Customers want information on exactly how a product or service will make a difference to their business.

Fortunately, both damaging habits can be fixed. The first step is to name a Chief Marketing Officer (CMO)—either an existing internal resource or a fractional C-suite resource. The second step is to identify a senior salesperson (VP Sales)—again, either an existing internal resource or a fractional C-suite resource. The third step is to give marketing responsibility for sales because of the CMO's strategic and customer-driven focus. Having completed these steps, the client company will be better prepared to address a lack of product knowledge by centralizing content development to guarantee a uniform message and creation of compelling value propositions.

Sales Challenges

The corporate sales process is among the top challenges faced by modern sales organizations. It is almost impossible to identify every challenge that a company's sales force encounters in their efforts to meet quota and makes sales. However, the following items would make anyone's top-ten list of common challenges.

1. Disjointed Sales Processes

Some variability is unavoidable, but lead generation, basic sales methodology, and how customers are brought into and guided through the system should all be standardized and documented so everyone handles them the same way. While it may not be easy, application of the appropriate technology and training can ensure that all activities flow into one stream where fulfillment, customer service, upselling, and other factors fit seamlessly into the whole, no matter the product or how it's sold.

2. Product Management and Marketing Alignment

This may be the most common challenge sales people face. Customers expect them to deliver exactly what marketing promised, which generates problems when marketing promises one thing and operations produces something different. Even when the product does exactly what the customer needs, they may feel disappointed because sales didn't give them what they expected.

Bringing marketing in on the common sales process can help align that function with reality. The marketing personnel will learn to market what the sales people are selling. Operations must participate as well, so sales and marketing can be absolutely sure of what they're selling. Otherwise, the cognitive discord between these essential groups can shatter the company.

3. Focus

The average salesperson wastes too much time on unimportant issues. Confusion, misguided cost-cutting efforts, noise, false opportunities, and poor self-discipline result in many spending less than half their time selling. A company can address these issues with a few solutions:

- Delegate. Lean on the talented people in your sales support departments instead of doing things yourself. Stop doing non-selling activities. Push low-value items as far down the hierarchy as possible, encouraging your team members to do the same.

- Filter. Use dashboards, scoreboards, and other tech-tools to put important metrics where everyone can see them. With the rise of ubiquitous online connectivity, it can be relatively easy for anyone anywhere to "keep score" and focus on their profitable tasks.

- Self-Control. Encourage your sales force to cut themselves off from distractions and reinforce self-discipline. This may mean taking fewer breaks and no longer checking personal social media during work hours. Coach team members to tighten self-control.

4. Technology

A company can't remain competitive in today's marketplace without up-to-date technology. At the same time, constant updates and new programs can confuse people. Smoothly adopting new technology requires careful analysis of the pros and cons, and a high level of focus to push it through. It also requires consistent training for all involved.

The process will soon break down, for example, if only three people in the company know how to use a mission-critical program, or if no one can access his/her sales metrics without fumbling through a steep learning curve. Spend the time and money necessary to train sales in new technology and the company will enjoy a smooth adoption.

5. Talent

In the *Scaling to Exit* program it is the responsibility of the internal, and/or fractional C-suite, learning & development function to ensure that sales reps receive experiential training and on-the-job coaching, preferably side by side with the content-development team. Sales representatives need to know how their products or services can solve customer problems. A successful sales strategy conveys this so that the sales force spends time targeting the correct customers at the right time.

Sales reps need to be knowledgeable and add value when they make customer contact, so strategy and infrastructure notwithstanding, it is absolutely key that the client company makes certain to hire good one(s). At the various stops in my career I have had great sales people, and I have had terrible sales people. I learned that a good sales person can make your company a success. I also learned that a good sales person is free! Let me give you a great example.

Earlier in my career, I worked for a publicly traded federal government contractor in the greater Washington, DC, area. I was the vice president and general manager (VP/GM) of our Systems Integration Division—a $20 million business unit. One of my division's largest contracts was with the General Services Administration, Public Building Service (GSA/PBS). The contract was to provide IT and systems integration support for the federal government's real estate arm (PBS) responsible for providing workspace to more than 1 million federal civilian workers and overseeing the preservation of more than 480 historic buildings. More than one hundred employees supported this contract.

At the end of the fourth year of the contract, it came up for re-compete; however, the follow-on contract had been set-aside for small business by the GSA. In other words, my company was not eligible to re-compete for the contract because we exceeded the size standards of the RFP. Suddenly, I was staring down the possibility of losing one hundred people and more than half of my divisional revenue. This type of thing happens to federal government contractors that generate 100 percent of their revenues through federal civilian agencies and the DoD (Department of Defense). It was a huge issue for us because the federal government contracting sales cycle was running twelve to eighteen months. It would be impossible for us to secure a replacement contract in time.

I brought my senior people together, and collectively we made a decision to pursue commercial contracts as a way to retain our workforce and backfill revenue. My company had come into existence as one of the early "beltway" contractors, and we were quite adept at business development in anticipation of writing responses to federal RFPs. As a company, we had absolutely no experience with sales (i.e., walking into a meeting with a potential client and coming out with a purchase order). Our "sales" department was of no use to us in this new strategy. I was forced to hire a sales person experienced in direct B2B sales.

The first sales person I hired spent the first two weeks in the office getting "acclimated." By the fourth week I had let him go for his lack of activity and progress. The second and third hires were more of the same. I was frustrated and beginning to panic because I was "burning so much daylight." I shared my frustration with a friend from church who was a VP of sales for a major software company. He wanted to know the type of questions I was asking in the interviews, because he felt that this might be the source of disconnect.

I shared my typical interview questions with him, and he told me that I was missing one important question. He told me that at the conclusion of the interview, I should ask the interviewee, in a very matter-of-fact manner, if they could be doing anything else with their life, what would it be? He told me that if they responded with anything but "I am a sales person," don't hire them. I took his advice and tried that approach. You wouldn't believe some of the responses that I got—everything from a sous chef to an opera singer.

After weeks of unsuccessful interviews, I finally interviewed a fellow who responded to the question with, "my great-grandfather was a salesman; my grandfather was a salesman; my father was a salesman…I was born to be a salesman." I hired him on the spot. To make a long story less long, this gentleman ended up being an incredible hire. He was so prolific that my division ended up representing 10 percent of the revenues and 30 percent of the profits for the entire company. This sales person rescued my division and made us a huge success, and he paid for himself so many times over that he was basically "free."

There are three really important lessons that came out of that experience, and those lessons have contributed mightily to my future successes with hiring important resources:

1. Hire the person; don't just fill the job. Far too many people are hired just to fill a position. A better approach is to make sure the person's skills and attitude are a good fit for the tasks at hand. Sure, it

may take longer to find the right person, but in the short and long run, it is worth it.

2. Fire quickly, including highly paid resources. Owners and managers are quick to terminate lower-level employees, but are far too generous in overlooking terminations that need to occur with higher-level resources.

3. Network with others. Never allow yourself to think you're the only one who understands the needs of your business. Wise owners tap into the insights and knowledge of other people so that everyone can benefit.

Conclusion

The purpose of the program is to scale EBITDA in order to double the valuation and increase the attractiveness of our client companies. A sustainable competitive advantage is very attractive to a potential buyer, and if the owner is the primary sales person, that does not equate to a sustainable competitive advantage. It is really important for owners to understand that, in this business environment, the only advantage a company will be able to create long-term is through its employees. It begins with the owner being a person with whom others want to associate.

In terms of sales people, the best rainmakers usually aren't looking for a job, but those are precisely the people a company should want. We encourage our client companies to hire a headhunter and offer prospects a better package selling a better product. Remember that top sales people already make a ton of money, so offering more money isn't good enough. You'll need to support their growth by identifying their professional and personal goals and being the organization to make it come to life.

Six

The Business-Purchase Process

This chapter is not intended to be comprehensive, nor should it be received as legal and/or tax advice. Every business transaction is unique, and sellers should always consult with a CPA and an attorney when considering a business sale structure to make certain all information is available, correct, transparent, and advantageous.

This segment was written from the perspective of the buyer of your business. It is really helpful to anticipate the questions that you—the seller—will be asked and the documents that you will need to produce. Most business owners are challenged with pulling all of this information together in a very compressed timeframe. The business owner who is emerging from the *Scaling to Exit* program, however, will have answers to all of the common questions and a database containing all of the documents that are included in a normal request. More importantly, the business owner emerging from the program will be confident that his/her company is healthy and attractive enough to receive the best possible purchase offers.

Before getting started

Early on in the business sell process, a preliminary valuation will be performed for your company. You will need to decide, based upon this preliminary valuation, whether the proceeds from the sale of the company will be sufficient to meet your current financial needs or fund your retirement. Obviously, you cannot make this determination without having a really good idea as to what your number is. For this reason, I would recommend that you meet with a financial advisor well in advance of initiating a business sell transaction. A financial advisor can assist you in determining how much money you will need to fund your vision for your financial future. Armed with this information, you can accurately assess adequacy of the preliminary valuation towards meeting your future financial needs.

It is important to know what your number is. It is even more important for you to know what you want to be after you sell your company. This is a point that was made in the introductory chapter of this book. It is so important that I felt compelled to re-visit here at the end. Just as you would see fit to engage a financial professional to help you to plan out your financial future, I would recommend that you engage a professional to help you plan what you will be after you sell your company.

Remember the fact that "the seller had a change of heart…" is far and away the number one reason that business sell transactions "go south". A change of heart that can be traced back to the owner's emotional attachment to their business. This would suggest that the most important exit plan is the plan for what you are going to be after you exit!

Overview of the Process

The business sell process can be broken down into two timeframes – pre-LOI (Letter of Intent) and post-LOI. The emphasis is on pre-LOI activities in the *Scaling to Exit* program, because the quality of the post-LOI experience between the parties is most often contingent upon the quality of the pre-LOI experience. We leverage our proprietary web technology to work hand-in-hand with your intermediaries to keep pre-LOI friction to an absolute minimum.

Each deal is different, but the graphic below depicts the usual pre-LOI work flow –

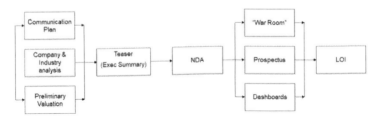

First Things First—Assess

The first thing a potential buyer is going to do is bring in a CPA, broker, and attorney to perform some due diligence on your company. The buyer wants to get a very clear sense of the business's strengths and weaknesses. Every transaction is different, but the buyer may begin by requesting a "business plan" that contains the following:

- Executive summary
- Description of your business
    - Value proposition (differentiators)
    - Key investment considerations for a buyer
    - Summary financials
- Proposed transaction structure
- Industry overview
- Company overview
    - History of your business
    - Marketing and sales organization
    - Operations
- Competitive landscape
- Summary of competition and your market position
- Management
- Your timetable for the transaction

Next—Valuation

Based on a review of the business plan, the buyer will make a decision to move forward or not. If the buyer decides to move forward, he or she will then want a valuation of your enterprise. The buyer's team is most likely to employ one of the following methods for assessing the value of your business. These methods help the buyer assess the current financial health of the business, as well as its growth potential.

1. Capitalized Earning

This is the equivalent of figuring out the expected return on investment (ROI). Generally, a mid-sized business will return 15–30 percent of the money spent purchasing it, and a good capitalization rate is 20–40 percent.

Here's how it works:

- Take the normal earnings of the business and project them forward, predicting the net present value of future earnings.

- Divide the future earnings by the capitalization rate (the risk comparison of buying this business versus investing in government bonds or long-term stocks).

In other words, the buyer is making certain that the acquisition of your business will return more money than a simple, stable, standard market investment. If it doesn't, the buyer will walk away from the deal.

2. Cash Flow

Under this method, the buyer is using cash flow as a proxy for understanding the business's ability to service debt, or, to grow in the future. With this valuation method, the buyer considers a balance of potential and risk, and determines if they can expect a gain if they sell the business five years down the line.

3. Tangible Assets

This method is pretty self-explanatory—the buyer values the business according to the value of its tangible assets, as listed on the balance sheet.

Balance sheets usually list fixed assets by their depreciated values, not the cost of replacement, so the buyer will certainly want to do some research (and some math) to make up the difference. This usually means the buyer will want a knowledgeable person to examine those assets and determine their wear and remaining lifespan.

Other Factors

There are a few things to keep in mind that will also influence the buyer's perception of your business's value:

- How badly do you want to sell the business?

  Selling the business because you have to sell the business (i.e., you have an illness) is an indicator to the buyer that he or she may be able to purchase the business for less than it is worth. Urgency caused by uncontrollable situations gives you less leverage in negotiations.

- How is the economy doing?

Experts expect 4 million businesses to hit the market in the next 3–5 years. Basic supply-and-demand theory suggests that sale prices on those businesses will be depressed. Only the best companies will be purchased for a premium valuation/sale price. Further, should an economic recession develop in that timeframe, it would exacerbate these realities.

- What does the industry look like?

  There is not much that you can do about your industry, but there is much that you can do to differentiate your business amongst others in the industry.

Once the buyer has determined a fair price for your business, he or she would be prepared to sign a Non-Disclosure Agreement (NDA) that prevents him/her from using the information you have provided for any purpose other than buying the business. They would also be prepared to submit a Letter of Intent (LOI), or Term Sheet, that essentially condenses the key elements of the sale into a single document.

The LOI should include the terms and conditions of the business sale, including payment, responsibilities, and period of confidentiality. Most importantly, the LOI will act as a timetable towards completion: explaining to each party the time-scale and deadlines for every step of the deal, from financing to the release of payments. The LOI helps prevent misunderstandings and avoids having to renegotiate any key terms close to the sale date.

The NDA and LOI combine to allow the transaction to move into preliminary due diligence.

SCALING TO EXIT 104

Preliminary Financial and Legal Due Diligence

During the next phase of the process, the buyer will conduct an in-depth financial and legal review of your business. During this review, he or she may request the following items:

- 2–3 years of financial statements
  - Balance Sheets
  - Income Statements
  - Cash Flow Statements

  Note: If you are able to have an experienced CPA pass along an audit letter with these documents, it strengthens their validity significantly.

- 2–3 years of income tax returns
- List of assets with estimated value
- Top customer list
- List of debt
- List of employees, including a breakdown of salaries and years of service
- Bank account information
- Business entity information
- CAP Table
- List of partners, subsidiaries, joint ventures

If, following preliminary due diligence, the deal and terms remain intact, the buyer will commence in-depth due diligence. During this stage, the buyer will likely add a valuation specialist to the existing CPA/broker/attorney team in order to perform a more thorough analysis of your business's accounts, practices, and day-to-day operations.

In-depth Due Diligence—How the Deal Will Be Structured

By the time that the transaction gets to in-depth due diligence, all parties will begin to consider how the deal should be structured. Whether the buyer will acquire the assets or the stock (or other equity interests) of your company will impact virtually every aspect of the deal. The type of transaction structure agreed upon between you and the buyer will dictate the contents of the definitive purchase agreement.

If your business is a sole proprietorship, a partnership, or a limited liability company (LLC), the transaction cannot be structured as a *stock* sale since none of these entity structures have stock. Instead, you can sell your partnership or membership interests. If the business is incorporated, either as a regular C-corporation or as a sub-S corporation, you and the buyer must decide whether to structure the deal as an *asset* sale or a *stock* sale.

Deciding whether to structure the sale as an *asset* sale or a *stock* sale is complicated because you and the buyer benefit from different structures. Generally, your buyer will prefer *asset* sales, whereas you will prefer *stock* sales. This segment does not address the tax implications of pursuing an *asset* deal versus a *stock* deal; however, the choice of structure often is driven by tax consideration that are complex and deal-specific. Involving tax counsel and accounting advisors early in the process, ideally before negotiating a letter of intent, can save you time and money in the long run.

Asset Sale

An asset-sale transaction involves the sale of some or all of the assets of your business. The purchased assets often encompass all or substantially all of the assets of the company; other times, the transferred assets include only those used in a specific division or certain selected assets of your company. In an asset deal, typically the buyer will assume only certain specified liabilities of your business.

A benefit of an asset sale is that it allows the parties significant flexibility as to what assets and liabilities are included in the transaction. In particular, for the buyer this is an opportunity to reduce his/her risk of assuming unknown liabilities associated with your business. Additionally, an asset sale allows a buyer to avoid spending money on unwanted assets. Sellers generally prefer a stock sale to an asset sale, but there may be instances where it would be ideal for you to be able to dispose of just a portion of your holdings. Asset sales often are used in connection with the sale of a distressed business, the sale of a business division, or in transactions where there are significant concerns about known and unknown liabilities.

For you as a seller, asset sales generate higher taxes because while intangible assets, such as goodwill, are taxed at capital gains rates, other "hard" assets can be subject to higher ordinary income tax rates. Federal capital gains rates are currently 20 percent, and state rates vary. Ordinary income tax rates depend on the seller's tax bracket. Furthermore, if the entity sold is a C-corporation, you as the seller will face double taxation. The corporation is first taxed upon selling the assets to the buyer. Then you, as the corporation's owner, are taxed again when the proceeds transfer outside the corporation. If your company is an S-corporation that was formerly a C-corporation, and if the sale is within the ten-year built-in gains (BIG) tax-recognition period, the S-corporation's asset sale could trigger corporate-level BIG taxes, under IRS Sec. 1374.

Stock Sale

A stock or equity-sale transaction involves the sale of the equity interests in your company from your equity holders to the buyer. In a stock deal, instead of choosing specific assets and liabilities to acquire, the buyer purchases an ownership stake in your entire business. In effect, the buyer acquires the entity instead of acquiring the business from the entity.

Sellers favor a stock sale because then all of the known and unknown liabilities of the business are transferred to the buyer, and therefore the seller may avoid ongoing exposure to such liabilities (other than as expressly agreed upon with the buyer). Buyers often resist a stock-sale transaction unless the company has a clean operating history or there are significant practical difficulties in completing an asset sale, such as restrictions on the transfer of certain assets from the selling company to the buyer or burdensome third-party consents required to transfer assets.

Though this segment has used the term "stock sale" to describe the primary alternative to an asset sale, it should be noted that another common M&A transaction structure, a merger, provides an alternative to a stock sale or asset sale. A merger is, in many ways, similar to a stock deal in that the buyer acquires the entire entity, including all of the assets and liabilities of the business. However, if the company has a significant number of stockholders, the stockholders are not easily accessible, or there is a risk that all of the stockholders will not support the transaction, then a merger may be preferable to a stock sale. This is due to the fact that a stock sale requires each and every stockholder to agree to sell the equity, while a merger usually requires approval of less than all of the stockholders. There are other considerations, including tax considerations, to attend to in opting for a merger instead of a stock sale, so it is really important to have counsel from knowledgeable and experienced legal and tax advisors.

Which Type of Sale Is the Most Prevalent?

Based on an analysis of marketplace transactions from the Pratt's Stats database, approximately 30 percent of all transactions are stock sales. However, this figure varies significantly by company size, with larger transactions having a greater likelihood of being stock sales.

Documents Required for In-depth Financial Due Diligence

- 5 years of financial statements
- 5 years of income tax returns
- Complete customer list
- Real property list
  - Owner property (deed)
  - Leased property (lease agreement)
- 2 years of payroll
- Insurance policies (liability, D&O, workers comp)
- Employee benefits plans (health, 401K, stock options, etc.)
- Bank statements
- Promissory notes/ mortgages
- Asset encumbrances

Documents Required for In-depth Legal Due Diligence

<u>Corporate documents</u>

- Shareholder/ Operating Agreement
- Meeting minutes
- Subsidiary/ Partnership/ JV arrangements
- Securities documents (certificates, warrants, options)

<u>Finance documents</u>

- Buy/Sell Agreements
- Promissory notes
- Convertible-debt documents
- Bank LOC agreements

<u>Operations documents</u>

- Supplier/ vendor contracts
- Raw-material-supplier agreements
- Manufacturing arrangements
- Company processes and specifications
- Company policies and procedures

<u>Sales and Marketing documents</u>

- Service/ product-sales agreements
- License agreements
- Consulting agreements
- Warranties/ guarantees

<u>Employment documents</u>

- Organization chart
- Employee files

- Employment agreements, non-competes, resumes
- Claims, disputes, disciplinary records
- Severance agreements

• Employee Handbook

Management (Officers, Directors, Partners, Managers) documents

• Agreements
• Questionnaires (pre-investment, public companies)
• Compensation (salary, bonus, stock options)
• Insider transactions
• Employment/ Non-compete/ Non-solicit agreements

Intellectual Property

• Copies of patents, trademarks, copyrights (registered and unregistered)
• Trade secrets
• Trade names/ dba's (state and federal)
• Websites/ domain names
• Software source code

Other

• Audits/ Litigation (IRS, state)
• Government Filings (SEC, state blue sky)
• Other material contractual obligations

An astute buyer (and all lower mid-tier buyers are astute) will use the available government databases to verify that all information provided is correct and accurate. These searches will show, for example, whether there are any liens on the business assets, whether there are unpaid taxes, whether there are ongoing lawsuits or human-rights complaints, and whether you own certain buildings or motor vehicles. Full transparency in every aspect of the sales process is paramount.

Closing

The terms have been agreed upon, the deal structure has been successfully negotiated, and all due diligence is complete. It's time to close on the sale. The following is a list of the legal documents that will be presented at closing. The various documents build on the content of the LOI and include, as efficiently as possible, the significant details of what you and the buyer are actually agreeing to. To the greatest extent possible, they also anticipate situations where things may not go as planned.

Final Documents

- APA, SPA—disclosure schedules from due diligence (Asset Purchase Agreement, Stock Purchase Agreement)
- Bill of Sale
- Subscription Agreement (Stock)
- Assignment & Assumption Agreement (General, IP)
- Financing documents
- Non-Compete/ Non-Solicitation Agreement
- Consulting Services Agreement (in instances where you as seller stay on)
- Settlement Statement
- Asset Acquisition Statement—IRS Form 8594

Conclusion

It sounds almost too good to be true that you can engage an extremely capable team to execute a powerful plan for scaling and selling your business, but history has repeatedly validated Victor Hugo's famous words, which I paraphrase as, "Nothing is stronger than an idea whose time has come."

Your success will not be the result of amazing luck or good fortune. Your success will be the result of engaging knowledgeable and experienced resources to execute the highly effective program articulated in this book.

I am reminded of an occasion twenty years ago when I played golf with my insurance agent. After I unceremoniously hit another ball into the woods, he asked me why I always pinched off the end of my swing. I responded that I was trying to prevent my ball from going into the woods. He gently suggested that since my ball goes into the woods anyway, why don't I "just let my hands go." He adjusted my grip, re-arranged my feet, and moved the ball up in my stance. Then he said, "now... just let your hands go and hit through the ball." I followed his plan and freely swung the club all the way through. I was amazed at the result.

To this day, when I play golf, I take a full, smooth swing at the ball. It still goes into the woods from time to time, but most of the time it goes a long way towards the hole. I share this story because it is an example of the great things that can happen when you pair strong counsel with a willingness to see a thing all the way through. The Baby Boomer looking to exit in the next 3–5 years can worry about what may go wrong and not take a full swing at his or her financial future, or he or she can focus on the good that will happen when he or she lets his/her hands go.

Appendix

The Fractional C-suite

A business owner who is embarking on an aggressive valuation-doubling exit strategy may not have the cash flow to hire all the required resources. A few experienced fractional resources in the C-suite can accelerate growth by providing strategy and planning for a specific function within the company. Clients in the *Scaling to Exit* program are operating on a tight 3–5 year plan; as a result, there is very little room for error and distraction. Our fractional executives fill gaps in C-suite roles—CMO, CFO, CTO, CIO, COO, etc.—in order to be catalysts to jump-start growth. This staffing strategy drives the creation of best practices for the client company that will be implemented by in-house staff for years to come. It also has a dramatic impact on the attractiveness of the company to potential buyers.

How Does It Work?

Fractional executives in the *Scaling to Exit* program have multiple clients. They typically commute to the offices of a client company and spend 3–4 hours at a time on a regularly scheduled basis, based upon need. For example, our fractional Chief Financial Officer (CFO) may maintain a schedule that devotes Monday to Client A, Tuesday to Client B, Wednesday to Client C, and so on, so that client companies have the opportunity to plan for his/her availability. In some cases, the executive will work on a project basis at the client's office full-time for a short period.

Fractional Roles

Corporate Development

Median salary: **$184,446**

Corporate development refers to the planning and execution of project-management strategies to meet organizational growth objectives. The corporate development role is the game changer that makes the *Scaling to Exit* program so radical. The role virtually guarantees a successful implementation of the program.

The corporate development resource works with other senior management players, particularly the CEO, to determine the course the client company will take. Then the corporate development resource coordinates his/her efforts with those of the *Scaling to Exit* program support team to move the company in line with those goals.

A corporate development resource has a diverse, comprehensive background that includes financial modeling, mergers and acquisitions (M&A), business development, and financial analysis. Often the corporate development resource comes from a legal or investment-banking background, due to the complex contractual and valuation issues associated with many activities.

In the *Scaling to Exit* program, the kinds of activities falling under corporate development may include management-team recruitment, phasing in or out of markets or products, arranging strategic alliances, identifying and acquiring companies (M&A), securing corporate financing, divesting of assets or divisions, and management of intellectual property. These activities are often delegated by the CEO, so communicating effectively in person, in writing, and via phone, text, and email is vital.

Chief Executive Officer (CEO)

Median salary: **$205,593**

Generally, the CEO should own the vision and build the culture of the organization. Ultimately the CEO is responsible for the development and execution of the company's long-term strategy with a view to creating shareholder value. The CEO's leadership also entails being responsible for all day-to-day management decisions and for implementing the company's long- and short-term plans.

CEOs develop and communicate the company's vision to employees, shareholders, customers, and business partners. They act as a direct liaison between the board of directors and management of the company and communicate to the board on behalf of management. They also communicate on behalf of the company to government authorities, other stakeholders, and the public.

Because they are the highest-ranking member of the "C-suite", CEOs lead and evaluate the work of other C-level officers, developing their skills and ensuring that their work aligns with corporate strategy. In this capacity, they engage in key activities such as:

- Ensuring the Company is appropriately organized and staffed, and delegating the authority to hire and terminate staff as necessary to enable it to achieve the approved strategy
- Ensuring that expenditures of the Company are within the budget

- Assessing the principal risks of the Company and ensuring that these risks are being monitored and managed

- Ensuring effective internal controls and management information systems are in place

- Ensuring that the Company has appropriate systems to enable it to conduct its activities both lawfully and ethically

- Ensuring that the Company maintains high standards of corporate citizenship and social responsibility wherever it does business

- Keeping abreast of all material undertakings and activities of the Company and all material external factors affecting the Company

- Ensuring that the Directors are properly informed and that sufficient information is provided to the Board to enable the Directors to form appropriate judgments

- Ensuring the integrity of all public disclosure by the Company

Note: In the majority of the $10M–$100M companies that we have consulted with, CEO roles and responsibilities are not carried out on a consistent basis. Typically, CEOs in these companies are operating two, maybe three, levels below where they should be. As a result, it is virtually impossible for vision, strategy, and culture to receive the level of priority that is necessary to enable the company to double its valuation. The corporate development resource comes alongside the CEO and helps facilitate the execution of these important activities.

Chief Operating Officer (COO)

Median salary: **$185,897**

The role of the COO varies depending on the company, but generally speaking, the COO oversees business operations. Often times, when a company is experiencing fast growth, a founder will take on the title of COO and then hire a CEO with more experience.

The COO should complement and strengthen the CEO because the two jobs taken together will most certainly determine the success of the enterprise. The COO should fill in the CEO's blind spots and vice versa, so the COO role takes a different shape at different companies.

The COO is the second-in-command and often succeeds to the top position when the CEO steps down. COO duties overlap with those of the CEO, but the primary responsibility of the COO is to manage day-to-day operations by meeting with individual department heads. Depending on the size of the facilities, the COO may walk company floors daily to observe operations and the progress of projects first-hand. The COO may also promote deserving workers to department-head positions.

Unlike other C-level executive roles, such as the CFO, there are no COO professional standards, nor are there common expectations of the job across all organizations. Rather than possessing a single set of skills that can be easily identified in any business, COOs have to adapt to the environment.

Chief Financial Officer (CFO)

Median salary: **$168,129**

According to the Ernst & Young consultancy, the duties of the CFO are changing. While their main responsibility is managing the company's finances, they often must also contribute to operational decision-making. At an operational level, the CFO may manage a Controller, who has a team of clerks and accountants, and a team of financial analysts/managers.

In many smaller companies, financial managers contribute as controllers and financial reporters rather than C-level strategists. At this level, they often work in tandem with a bookkeeper or an accountant. As the company grows, the role expands to not only include overseeing the capital structure of the company, but also communicating with the rest of the C-suite to make sure their actions (pricing, budgeting, expenses) are financially prudent.

By the time a company is ready to double its valuation, there is a need for a CFO with the ability to effectively leverage financial risk. The financially risk-averse orientation that was appropriate during product development and proof of product/market-fit phases becomes an impediment to success in the pursuit of an increase in valuation. Calculated and prudent risk-taking becomes "safer" than not taking any risk at all, particularly where the prospect of large returns warrants the additional risk. This is, in large part, why timely and actionable financial statements are so important.

Actionable Financial Statements

A big part of "fixing" a company is scouring through records. Most business owners live out of their business in order to decrease their tax liability, thus, many are running personal expenses and non-recurring expenses through their business (e.g., travel, meals, entertainment, repairs, etc.). In the buy-sell transaction, these are actually seller's discretionary earnings ("SDE")—defined as an estimate of the total financial benefit a full-time owner-operator would derive from the business on an annual basis. It is important to have someone go through all of the books and records and add those personal and non-recurring expenses back to the bottom line.

Accounting, and the financial reports that the accounting function produces, is the language of business. It tells a story about the dynamics of assets and liabilities within a company over time and under conditions of varying degrees of uncertainty and risk. So, naturally, the question that a buyer will ask in the initial assessment of risk is, "How good are the financials? Are they minimal or do they tell an in-depth story about the business?"

To perform a self-check on this issue, ask yourself the following questions:

- Can one easily track the flow of revenue and expenses from an invoice to the financials to the tax returns?

- Can one track the sales of the top five customers?

- Can one easily prove all of the perks that the owner(s) receives from the company?

Readily available commercial-off-the-shelf (COTS) accounting software will allow a company to provide this type of information and so much more. When a buyer is interested in a company, the ease with which the owner can prove the financial performance of his/her business has a direct impact on value. Incomplete or inaccurate financials communicate to the buyer that no one is watching and tracking the company's performance, and, therefore, future performance (of real importance to the buyer) is unpredictable. Value is created or destroyed by the ease with which one can see the company's future, as told through timely and actionable financial statements.

It is important to note that an informed reader of financial reports will gain varied levels of comfort based on the type of financial statements provided. The three general levels of financial-statement services are *audit*, *review*, and *compilation*.

- An *audit* is the highest level of financial-statement service a CPA can provide.

- A *review* provides limited assurance, and should be the minimal level of financial-statement service that a seller engages in with a CPA.

- In a *compilation*, the CPA expresses no assurance about the accuracy of the financial statements presented. In fact, the report attached to the financial statement emphasizes that the service is a compilation. This is the typical level of financial-statement service that a CPA provides to small- and medium-sized businesses in tax preparation.

A normal clause in a purchase agreement for a business is that, to the best of the owner's knowledge, the financial statements are true and correct. Obviously, audited financials lend the most credibility to that representation.

Chief Marketing Officer (CMO)

Median salary: **$163,961**

The CMO is the interface between a company and its customers. CMOs are responsible for marketing operations, marketing communication, and customer-relationship management. CMOs are also responsible for meeting the revenue and growth targets of their company. In other words, they have a critical role in ensuring that product development and sales are focused on meeting the needs of customers. In their operational role, CMOs typically manage a team of marketing specialists and plan campaigns in collaboration with external marketing resources.

The *Scaling to Exit* fractional CMO employs a variety of sales and marketing best practices in a bid to generate hyper-revenue growth and the following collateral impacts:

- Recurring revenue
- Revenue diversity (more customers that generate smaller percentages of overall revenue)
- Repeat customers
- Low attrition

It has been our observation that very few small businesses have a formal, consistent marketing line item on their budget. Those small businesses that do have a marketing budget typically fail to base that number on a solid rationale by considering what's normal in their industry, how much their competitors spend, and other relevant factors. In order for a firm to double its valuation, a professionally designed and implemented marketing strategy is critical.

Once a company has established product/market fit, it is time to grow. To this end, one of the smartest things a mid-market company can do is source a competent CMO to develop an executable marketing strategy that will set the company apart from the competition. Marketing is the only way to get more exposure for a company's brand and the only reliable long-term strategy to attract more business to it. Marketing success is defined in terms of the amount of business generated by a specific level of marketing spend. As long as the ROI is positive, the marketing spend pays for itself. The majority of small businesses neglect marketing strategies, restrict spending, and ultimately limit potential.

General Counsel (GC)

Median salary: **$182,919**

The GC or Chief Legal Officer (CLO) is an expert and leader who helps the company minimize its legal risks by advising the company's other officers and board members on any major legal and regulatory issues the company confronts, such as litigation risks.

The GC will advise the business when changes are made to the laws and also sets up training on legal matters for employees, when applicable. In addition, the GC is often responsible for investigating issues of non-compliance and suggesting measures to take if non-compliance starts to become a bigger issue. In cases where a business is involved in a lawsuit, the GC may act as the chief litigator.

Chief Human Resources Officer (CHRO)

Median salary: **$155,574**

The human resources (HR) function for firms of fewer than 50 employees tends to be short term (hiring, firing, promoting) and transactional, with an appropriate emphasis on benefits, payroll, and compliance. On the run to doubling valuation, the HR function must become much more strategic. Working closely with the CEO, the CHRO supports company culture and implements staff-development programs. Once talent is found, it has to be nurtured and sufficiently leveraged to help the company grow.

There is an overwhelming demand for high-performing talent in today's market place. As companies pursue the doubling of their valuation, they must compete with much larger firms for the best and brightest people. The CHRO plays a critical role in helping the organization figure out how to identify, attract, develop, and grow the talent it needs to succeed.

Interestingly, many of today's most effective CHROs come from non-HR backgrounds, such as finance, operations, or legal. Individuals from these disciplines tend to be assertive and data-driven leaders who take a stance on talent issues and use relevant facts to deliver a talent strategy for their organization. Effective CHROs take direct responsibility for contributing to business performance and driving revenue growth. The executive team values them for their business acumen more than for their technical human-resources skills.

Chief Learning Officer (CLO)

Median salary: **$152,563**

The advent of the CLO has been fairly recent, and CLO tasks are often the most overlooked by companies seeking to double valuation. A knowledgeable and experienced

CLO will enable the company to scale to meet the demands of CMO-generated growth.

There is still much debate about what the CLO role encompasses. For our purposes, the CLO oversees the implementation of a strategy to accomplish three extremely important tasks:

1. Define the company's value stream; then identify, document, and train on the repeatable processes required to move product/services across the value stream as quickly and efficiently as possible.

2. Equip the executive team with the leadership skills that will be required to scale the enterprise.

3. Equip the entry- to mid-level managers with the basic blocking and tackling skills that they will need to help the company scale.

Chief Information Officer (CIO)

Median salary: **$181,271**

CIOs are responsible for the company's information-technology strategy and operations. They work closely with other C-level executives to ensure that there is an information-technology strategy in place and that it is aligned with the company's core business strategy. The CIO is also responsible for the digitized technology and computer systems that support the company's mission and help it scale. As a member of the executive team, the CIO has to inspire employees to embrace technology and systems, and he/she must manage any resistance to change.

The CIO role becomes critical as a company grows and becomes more decentralized geographically. More assets are stored, accessed, and distributed electronically, and more work is being done in a cloud environment. On the one hand, cloud computing can reduce the company's IT infrastructure and management costs and make the company more agile and responsive to changing market conditions. On the other hand, cloud computing immediately introduces concerns about systems security and company-sensitive information being leaked.

I have been involved with information technology for more than thirty years, and I can't remember a time when there was so much change happening at such a rapid pace in so many parts of the technology landscape. Mobile, data, the cloud—these and other technologies are changing at incredible speed. Any attempt by a company to double its valuation without the assistance of a CIO is futile in today's connected marketplace.

Chief Technology Officer (CTO)

For some companies it is appropriate to include a Chief Technology Officer in addition to, or in the place of, a CIO. The CTO is an executive who is responsible for the management of an organization's research and development (R&D) and technological needs. A chief technology officer (CTO) considers all technology needs of a business and deploys capital to make investments towards the achievement of an organization's goals. Companies that focus on scientific and electronic products employ CTOs who are responsible for the oversight of intellectual property and have backgrounds in the specific industries in which they operate.

End Notes

Introduction

Rabbi Hillel quote:
Hillel, *Pirke Avot* I.14, translated Charles Taylor;
Ethics of the Fathers 1:14

Jerry Garcia quote:
Paumgarten, Nick. "Deadhead: The afterlife." *The New Yorker*, November 26, 2012
https://www.newyorker.com/magazine/2012/11/26/dea dhead.

Chapter 1

Stanley, Thomas J. *The Millionaire Next Door: The Surprising Secrets of America's Wealthy.* Lanham, MD: Taylor Trade Publishing, 1996.

Stanley, Thomas J. *The Millionaire Mind.* Kansas City: Andrews McMeel Publishing, 2001.

Hemingway quote:
While no precise citation has been discovered for the quote that is widely attributed to Hemingway, some scholars and fans have suggested a story entitled "Blood Sport" by Ken Purdy, which originally appeared in the July 27, 1957 edition of the *Saturday Evening Post*. In this story the following quotation appears: "'There are three sports,' she remembered Helmut Ovden saying. 'Bullfighting, motor racing, mountain climbing. All the rest are recreations.'" It has been noted that the character of Helmut Ovden is modeled after Ernest Hemingway. This is one explanation of why the quote has been so widely attributed to Hemingway. For more information, see:

https://web.archive.org/web/20120203013838/http://w
ww.timelesshemingway.com/content/quotationsfaq

Chapter 2

Koch, Richard. *The 80/20 Principle: the Secret of Achieving More with Less.* New York: Doubleday, 1998.

Collins, Jim. *Good to Great: Why Some Companies Make the Leap... and Other Don't.* New York: Harper Business, 2001.

Dwight D. Eisenhower. Address at the Second Assembly of the World Council of Churches, Evanston, Illinois. *August 19, 1954*
http://www.presidency.ucsb.edu/ws/?pid=9991

"There's only you and me and we just disagree."
    Dave Mason, "We Just Disagree," *Let It Flow*, 1977

Carroll, Lewis. *Alice's Adventures in Wonderland.* Basingstoke, United Kingdom: Macmillan Publishers, 1865.

Chapter 3

MacKay, Harvey. *Dig Your Well Before You're Thirsty.* New York: Currency Books, 1999.

Brandon Hall Group's 2016–2017 Training Benchmarking Study, available at http://www.brandonhall.com

Charan, Ram, Stephen Drotter, and James Noel. *The Leadership Pipeline: How to Build the Leadership-Powered Company.* San Francisco: Jossey-Bass, 2001.

Statistics and data in this chapter sourced from:
    Sanders, G I. "Employee Productivity Statistics: Every Stat You Need to Know." Dynamic Signal. 2001.

https://dynamicsignal.com/2017/04/21/employee-productivity-statistics-every-stat-need-know/.

Flade, Peter, Jim Asplund, and Gwen Elliot. "Employees Who Use Their Strengths Outperform Those Who Don't." Gallup. http://news.gallup.com/businessjournal/186044/employees-strengths-outperform-don.aspx.

Dvorak, Nate, and William Kruse. "Managing Employee Risk Requires a Culture of Compliance." Gallup. http://news.gallup.com/businessjournal/190352/managing-employee-risk-requires-culture-compliance.aspx .

Katz, Eyal. "Remote Workforce NPS: The Most Important Metric You're Missing." Business 2 Community. https://www.business2community.com/business-innovation/remote-workforce-nps-important-metric-youre-missing-01785305#oWRIA4bsxOwz6011.97.

Harter, Jim. "Companies Are Maximizing Only 5% of Their Workforces." Gallup. http://news.gallup.com/businessjournal/182087/companies-maximizing-workforces.aspx.

Witters, Dan, and Sangeeta Agrawal. "Well-Being Enhances Benefits of Employee Engagement." Gallup. http://news.gallup.com/businessjournal/186386/enhances-benefits-employee-engagement.aspx.

Cvent Study, available at https://www.colloquy.com/loyalty-strategies/for-loyal-customers-look-to-your-employees/

Chapter 4

Park, Chang. "Maximize the Return on Your Advertising Spend." Nielsen.

http://www.nielsen.com/us/en/insights/news/2009/ma
ximize-the-return-on-your-advertising-spend.html.

The CMO Survey, https://cmosurvey.org

Leone, Chris. "What is a Good Marketing ROI?"
WebStrategies.
https://www.webstrategiesinc.com/blog/what-is-a-good-
marketing-roi.

Chapter 5

Boaz, Nate, Murnane, John, Nuffer and Nuffer, Kevin.
"The Basics of Business-to-Business Sales Success."
McKinsey & Company.
https://www.mckinsey.com/business-
functions/marketing-and-sales/our-insights/the-basics-of-
business-to-business-sales-success.

Chapter 6

Pratt's Stats, available at
https://www.bvresources.com/products/pratts-stats

Victor Hugo quote
    Original Language: On résiste à l'invasion des armées;
on ne résiste pas à l'invasion des idées. {*Histoire d'un
Crime* (The History of a Crime) [written 1852, published
1877], Conclusion, ch. X. Trans. T.H. Joyce and Arthur
Locker}
    Literal translation: One resists the invasion of armies;
one does not resist the invasion of ideas.

About the Author

Michael Watkins is the founder and president of The Alchemy Group. It has been his mission to assist organizations in their efforts to transform themselves into growing, profitable companies. His business acumen is the result of more than 30 years in senior executive roles in a variety of settings from publicly traded companies to technology start-ups. Those experiences created in him a passion for lower mid-market sized businesses, and the unique challenges that they face on a daily basis. Over time, he discovered that his client companies receive the best value and impact when his resources come along-side them. When his resources roll up their sleeves and join the client company in the trenches. This radically different approach to management consulting, which substitutes advice and counsel with task management and execution, is the foundation for the *Scaling to Exit* approach.

Michael's formal education includes – Juris Doctorate, University of Maryland School of Law; Masters of Business Administration, Finance, Hood College, and Bachelors of Arts, English, University of Rochester.

You can find out more about The Alchemy Group and about bringing the *Scaling to Exit* program to your company at www.scalingtoexit.com.

If you have any other questions or want any other help, call 1-970-660-8018 or email info@scalingtoexit.com.

Made in the USA
Lexington, KY
29 September 2018